CHINK

CHINK

THINKING BEYOND THE STEREOTYPE

HENRY WOONGJAE KONG

CHINK
THINKING BEYOND THE STEREOTYPE

iUniverse books may be ordered through booksellers or by contacting:

iUniverse
1663 Liberty Drive
Bloomington, IN 47403
www.iuniverse.com
1-800-Authors (1-800-288-4677)

Because of the dynamic nature of the Internet, any web addresses or links contained in this book may have changed since publication and may no longer be valid. The views expressed in this work are solely those of the author and do not necessarily reflect the views of the publisher, and the publisher hereby disclaims any responsibility for them.

Any people depicted in stock imagery provided by Thinkstock are models, and such images are being used for illustrative purposes only.
Certain stock imagery © Thinkstock.

ISBN: 978-1-5320-3547-0 (sc)
ISBN: 978-1-5320-3548-7 (hc)
ISBN: 978-1-5320-3546-3 (e)

Library of Congress Control Number: 2017917745

Print information available on the last page.

iUniverse rev. date: 01/27/2018

Dedicated to Emily and Andrew,
Twenty first century American Asians

Special thanks to Professor Elaine Kim for the Berkeley interview,
Deborah Treisman for helpful comments,
And Jessica Treisman for the editing, photography and much else

Contents

Preface

Flying into Vietnam on my first Asian holiday in twenty years, I naively believed that my Asian American background would somehow resonate in this land of fellow Asians. But amidst the throngs of frenzied merchants and chaotic mopeds in the Old Quarter of Hanoi, I quickly realized that I had nothing in common with these people. To them I was just another tourist, perhaps of the Chinese or Japanese variety, as opposed to the Europeans or Australians, all of whom were still greeted with the same standard Third World sales pitch: "come, you buy, good price, T-shirt, boat ride, coconut" in passable if broken English.

We Americans have our preconceptions of the Vietnamese, reflecting our wartime misadventures there a half century ago. Surely the Vietnamese must have their own preconceptions of us as well, molded by the incessant television shows and Hollywood movies we have exported so successfully to all corners of the world. But preconceptions tend to be annihilated on contact with reality. And the reality in these teeming Asian lands is the constant striving for survival and success in the global economy. It is no longer the struggle it must have been for earlier generations living in the shadows of war and post-colonial revolution, but rather a confident forward-looking endeavour, indifferent to the vicissitudes of history or ideology. The wars and revolutions eventually blur into the backdrop of centuries. These people have no time to hold grudges. There is too much living and working left to do!

So here in the heart of Southeast Asia, I realized that the issues of identity that have nagged me as the son of Korean immigrants do not apply to the vast majority of Asians. They know who they are and where they want to go. Nor do they apply to the Caucasian backpackers and tourists wandering the night markets and bars. They have come here to explore and exploit, not to go native. Whether Asian peoples succeed or fail will increasingly depend on them rather than on the interference of white peoples. And history has demonstrated time and again that Asians are their own worst enemy. But Asian Americans are not Asians. They have different *perceived affordances*, to borrow a rather obscure but apt term from cognitive psychology. For the Asian American who never felt that he truly belonged in the land of the white man, it is disconcerting to discover that he is a stranger in the land of familiar faces. Our sense of identity is informed more by shared tongue and taste than by the shape of our eyes.

My book is as much about identity and belonging as it is about stereotype and racism. They are in some ways flip sides of the same coin. We use stereotypes as shortcuts to identify others and we sometimes resort to racism as a quick and dirty way of confirming that we belong to the in-group. That is natural and universal in our species. Humans have evolved to belong. They have also evolved to exploit economic opportunity, even if it means uprooting themselves from their ancestral lands and settling down in alien cultures inhabited by different-looking people. The descendants of these immigrants have had to choose one of two paths: assimilation or self-segregation. The latter path naturally leads to marginalization and sometimes discrimination at the hands of the majority. But the former path is also fraught, for it means severing oneself from one's old cultural foundation while hoping for acceptance from a newly adopted one. This takes time, perhaps a generation or two.

I wrote this book for these generations in flux: those children and grandchildren of immigrants who are forgetting where they came from but don't yet know where they are going. This is something that most Asian Asians and white Americans cannot fully comprehend. What does it mean to be Asian in a Eurocentric world? Obviously generalization is dangerous when experience differs for everybody. But certain themes tend to recur in the greater Asian American experience. For example, the (often insulting) Hollywood depictions, the expectations for (and resentment of) academic achievement, and the asymmetrical sexual stereotypes of Asian men versus Asian women.

Asian Americans are the forgotten minority, overshadowed by the conflicts and crises involving African Americans and Hispanics. But with the rise of Asia on the geopolitical stage, and the growing numbers and prominence of Asian Americans, it is high time to take a critical look at this long neglected element of the so-called melting pot.

Henry Woong-jae Kong
Hanoi
August 2017

1

Me Love You Long Time
The Hollywood Asian

> If a man dwells on the past, then he robs the present. But if a man ignores the past, he may rob the future. The seeds of our destiny are nurtured by the roots of our past.
>
> Master Po
> *Kung Fu*

> No more yankie my wankie. The Donger need food!
>
> Long Duk Dong
> *Sixteen Candles*

The typecasting started almost as soon as I got off the plane at JFK in the summer of 1973. Cute little Asian, rice bowl hair, no English: perfect for the role. On the Saturday morning TV was *Hong Kong Phooey*: "number one super guy, Hong Kong Phooey, faster than the human eye, chicka chong, chika chong, chika chong chong chong." These were the days before it was politically incorrect to depict Asians as squinty-eyed mushrooms dancing in Disney cartoons. The kid across from me in homeroom sported a lunchbox with David Carradine's Shaolin master Kwai Caine squinting off into the distance. "Do you hear grasshopper?". "No I don't hear him", I replied earnestly. "Wise Shaolin master hear grasshopper." Little did we know that master Caine's superhuman hearing and wisdom wouldn't be enough to protect him from accidental autoerotic asphyxiation in a Bangkok hotel room 35 years later. In the playground, I was supposed to be Bruce Lee. But here things quickly went from sweet to sour. In the fifth grade, a group of bullies used to taunt me at the bus stop. I was the only Asian kid there, and no one stood up for me. "Hey, you know kung fu? You know karate? Show us kung fu, Jackie Chan!" They threatened bodily harm if I didn't perform. So I would cartwheel my arms a few times, do a low flying kick and yell, "hhhaaaiii-yyyaaa!" Laughter. They called my bluff. Soon after, they came up behind me in the bathroom and asked if I was a chink or a gook. After a moment's hesitation, I said quietly, "I'm a Korean". "Hey, hear that? Speak up. You a chink or gook?" "I'm a Korean," I replied again. "No, really? You a chink or gook? For real, chink or a gook, chink or gook?" I was no longer Bruce Lee, I was chinkergook.

Asians and their culture are still considered exotic by many Americans. People who haven't had the opportunity to meet many foreigners in person are unduly influenced by popular movies and the mass media. This is understandable. What's unfortunate is that Hollywood has been content to propagate and reinforce outdated stereotypes in place of accurate and sensitive portrayals. As an Asian American child growing all over the United States (including Mississippi, South Carolina, New York City, New Jersey, and California) during the 1970's, I too was brainwashed by Hollywood.

An enduring stereotype dating back to my childhood is that of the Asian woman. She usually comes in only one of two sensual flavors: the scheming seductress (warning: contents may be hot) or the fragile plaything (caution: handle with care). The first dates at least as far back as the treacherous *Daughter of Fu Manchu*, conjured up by the English writer Sax Rohmer in the 1920's. A recent reincarnation is the Lucy Liu character from the 90's sitcom *Ally McBeal*. In the show, Ms. Liu plays a domineering Mandarin-speaking lawyer who also happens to be well versed in dangerously erotic sexual techniques from the Orient (autoerotic asphyxiation, perhaps?). She knows how to keep the white men in line, begging for more. The role of the Asian dominatrix has come to be known as that of the "dragon lady". At the other end of the spectrum is the tragic *Cio-Cio San* character from Giacomo Puccini's opera *Madama Butterfly*. Among its many variations is the 1960 film, *World of Suzie Wong*, based on the novel by the Englishman Richard Mason, and the

Broadway musical *Miss Saigon*. Unlike dragon ladies, these China dolls are portrayed as victims of a misogynistic Oriental culture who need to be rescued (invariably by the dashing Caucasian leading man).

Sometimes a single character incorporates aspects of both dragon lady and China doll at once. In Stanley Kubrick's *Full Metal Jacket* (1987), American GI's hanging out on a Saigon street corner are approached by a strutting hooker whose entire English vocabulary seems to consist of a few choice phrases: *"hey you have girlfriend Vietnam? You wanna party? Me love you long time. Me so horny."* The brief encounter encapsulates the juxtaposition of dare and desire that proves viscerally irresistible to young men. Particularly disturbing is the notion that the identity of the Asian woman is intimately tied to what she can do for the pleasure of the white man. She is nothing but a faceless foil for the Western male psyche. For decades, the Hollywood imagination has been stuck in this dragon lady/ China doll dichotomy.

Demeaning stereotypes are by no means confined to the feminine sex. In some respects, Asian men have had it even worse. Here, too, we are faced with a degrading dichotomy. At one end of the spectrum is the Chinatown gangster played by Jet Li in *Lethal Weapon 2* (1989), while at the other is the emasculated nerd, immortalized by Gedde Watanabe's *Long Duk Dong* ("what's happenin', hotstuff?") in *Sixteen Candles* (1984). The Asian male is either a sadistic kung fu thug or a socially inept buffoon. Both are served as appetizers for the handsome and morally righteous white male lead, who in the end gets to consummate his carnal desire with a China doll.

The Hollywood Asian stereotype sprouts from two roots. First is the economic mindset of the men who produce these movies, and second is the evolutionary psychology of the folks who pay to watch them. The motion picture industry is a multi-billion dollar behemoth controlled by powerful producers and executives driven first and foremost by the profit margin. Almost all of them are men. Cultural sensitivity and moral responsibility take back seats behind the bottom line. Movie moguls are obsessed at figuring out what Mr. Smith at the multiplex will pay to see. Getting that right was what made them rich and successful in the first place. And the richer and more successful they become, the more likely they are to continue to produce the kind of movies that Mr. Smith will want to watch. In fact, these movies help Smith construct his own desires. Hollywood will then try to replicate and surpass its past successes, creating yet more demand. An unmistakable Darwinian logic lurks behind this self-propagating cycle.

There's a good chance that our Mr. Smith is actually a pimply teenager who's never been to Asia, and doesn't know the first thing about Confucius or Kung fu, but routinely fantasizes about the cute little Korean girl in his class. Or he may be a lonely vet who lost his virginity in an Asian brothel back in the last war. Either way, Hollywood producers know that Smith will gladly pay to watch scantly clad Asian girls seduce him on screen. After all, the essential promise of cinema is to transport the audience to a fantasyland for a few blissful hours.

Evolutionary psychology teaches us why we tend to have the fantasies we do. Like all mammals, biological constraint forces human beings to invest asymmetrically in the economics of child care. A female produces just a few hundred viable eggs in her reproductive lifetime, while males waste billions of sperm with each ejaculate. Women usually carry just a single embryo through nine months of gestation, culminating in the grueling and potentially fatal process of childbirth. They then spend years nursing and feeding each of their children. Men don't have to do any of this to be considered successful fathers. Donald Trump can proudly boast that he never changed a diaper in his life and still end up president.

Female reproductive resources are scarce. This is why males have been competing with one another, sometimes to the death, for sexual access to females over the course of evolutionary history. The optimal way for a man to pass on his genes is to impregnate as many women as often as possible, in the expectation that at least some of them would be willing to raise his progeny to sexual maturity. The ideal reproductive strategy for a woman, on the other hand, is to select the fittest man to be the father of her unborn child and the most dedicated husband to help her rear that child (the two need not be the same, much to the chagrin of cuckolds). Males and females who fail to follow this playbook are likely to leave fewer offspring. For men, it pays to play the field, while for women, it makes more sense to be picky. This fundamental difference in reproductive strategy was honed over the course of millions of years and hundreds of thousands of generational cycles of natural selection. It has molded the brains, minds, desires, and drives of men and women around the world. This is why male sexual fantasies tend to involve casual sex with multiple anonymous partners, while female fantasies are usually more emotionally elaborate affairs with a single partner.

A separate discovery from cognitive neuroscience is also relevant to our discussion. In response to anticipation, a chemical called *dopamine* is released by an ancient region deep in the brain called the *striatum*. Dopamine is a neurotransmitter that binds to receptors on nerve cells that project to another, more recently evolved part of the brain: the *prefrontal cortex*, the site of goal-directed decision coding. Dopamine serves as a fundamental molecular currency for both anticipation and its fulfillment. As more dopamine is released, both the expectation of reward and the pleasure one gets from it are increased. This explains why, among other things, sex feels so much better after a long tease.

A third point relates to the psychology of *in-group/out-group* morality, a topic I shall explore in more depth in the next chapter. People feel a greater sense of responsibility for their behavior amongst individuals with whom they share a common identity, be it race, language, politics, religion, or even favorite sports team. We naturally suppress our more selfish side when surrounded by like-minded individuals. But amongst strangers, this inhibition tends to break down, and people feel they can get away with behavior that might otherwise be unacceptable.

Putting these things together, we can see why the Hollywood portrayals of Asian women appeal to a white male audience. Men of all races fantasize about having unattached sex more than women do. China dolls are depicted as more receptive than independent white women, but conquering a dragon lady gets you an even bigger buzz. Asians are exotic creatures who live far away from the rules that govern mainstream white society. Film executives and advertising consultants have spent decades trying to understand the predilections of the movie going public, and they parlay their findings to produce goods designed to maximize profit in the marketplace of desires. The Hollywood Asian woman stereotype is a white male fantasy lurking at the crossroads of economics and evolutionary psychology.

Let's examine the Asian male through the same lens. Women have what men want, but it's in limited supply. In the struggle for access to Asian women, Asian men are, at best, nuisances to be brushed away or, at worst, mortal enemies to be exterminated. The emasculated buffoon Long Duk Dong is just one of a long line of asexualized/feminized Asian characters going back to the pig-tailed coolies rushing for gold in frontier California. These men and their gene pools were effectively removed from the competition. Not all Asians are so docile. Some must be eliminated with extreme prejudice. In *Rambo: First Blood Part 2* (1985), Sylvester Stallone plays a renegade Vietnam veteran who single-handedly dispatches legions of hapless Vietcong troops and rescues his Asiatic damsel from distress. While ostensibly dressed as Reagan-era jingoism (Rambo also destroys helicopter gunships full of Russians), the movie has an unmistakable undercurrent of racist xenophobia. Nearly a century of American military adventures in Asia provides a convenient pretext for showcasing the Asian male stereotype at its worst.

But what about feminine fantasy? Women make up half the movie-going population. It's hard to believe they have a particular desire to watch American GI's cavorting with Vietnamese hookers or Chinatown thugs being dismembered by white cops. It bears repeating here that Hollywood producers are largely men who best identify with other like-minded men. Incidentally, this is also true of the newer generation of Asian-American producer/directors such as Justin Lin, director of *Better Luck Tomorrow* (2003), whose films often portray Asian females in the same demeaning light.

There are, of course, female writers, producers, and directors, and their films do tend to be more female friendly: less violence and raunchy humor, more sensitive character development. But few of these movies have Asian themes. Two notable exceptions are *Joy Luck Club* (1993), directed by Wayne Wang based on the novel by Amy Tan, and *The Lover* (1992), a French production based on Marguerite Duras' semi-autobiographical novel. It's interesting to compare them with each other and with the much more numerous body of films targeted to the white male audience. *Joy Luck Club* was written by a Chinese-American woman, and it shows. All the protagonists are female (four pairs of mothers and daughters) whose characters are portrayed with sensitive nuance. No shallow China dolls or dragon ladies here. Unfortunately, the male Asian characters are not as well developed, and seem to take a back seat to the white men who try to capture the protagonists' hearts.

Set in colonial French Indochina, *The Lover* is an exquisitely sensual film about a wealthy Chinese playboy who has an affair with a sexually precocious but impoverished French teenager. In contrast to *Joy Luck Club,* there are no female Asian characters to speak of, but the male lead, played by the Hong Kong actor Tony Leung Ka-fai, is a multi-dimensional character whose virile exploits have no parallel in traditional Hollywood movies. The object of his desire, ravishingly played by the English actress Jane March, is an idealized sex object: a kind of European doll.

A major theme of my book is the universality of human nature. Every single one of us is a descendant of African Adam and Eve, who emerged out of a population bottleneck a hundred thousand years ago as two sexes and a single race. Sexual divergence was already a billion year old genetic fact, but racial divergence had yet to happen. Racial distinction, evolutionarily speaking, is insignificant compared to sexual distinction.

A second major theme is that cultural differences between populations are largely the result of environmental, rather than genetic, factors affecting subsequent political, economic, and military history. Six hundred years ago, East Asians, Arabs, and Europeans were roughly equal in terms of cultural sophistication. The most extraordinary collection of events in the intervening centuries was the economic/technological/military development of Western Europe. The annihilation of distance by fifteenth century Iberian conquistadors, the domestication of power by nineteenth century British industrialists, and the commodification of culture by twentieth century American advertisers conspired to tip the balance. It is this relatively recent historical legacy, and not some mysterious essence inherent in white skin, that now makes Hollywood far more influential than Bollywood. The East has been suffused by a Western *cultural field potential.*

If one accepts that the stereotypes of Asian men and women in Hollywood movies are driven by white male producers, then what can we predict from Asian cinema? My feeling is that because the universality of human nature predates the divergence of human cultures, the racial and sexual stereotypes of Asians in Western movies will simply be replaced by similar stereotypes of Caucasians in Asian movies. In other words, movies catering to largely male Asian audiences will objectify young white women as sexual playthings, either as adorable "arm candy" or devious gold diggers, and vilify white males as bumbling fools or mortal enemies. The "Hong Kong American" may turn out to be just a racist reversal of the Hollywood Asian. However, I think that in general, Asian stereotypes in Western cinema is more likely to be salient than the Western stereotypes in Asian cinema simply because of the deeply asymmetrical historical legacy of European cultural imperialism.

To be fair, there has been a welcome move towards inclusion, prompted perhaps in part as a reaction to the Motion Picture Academy's historical lack of appreciation for nonwhite actors. A notable example is the sitcom *Fresh Off the Boat*, loosely based on Eddie Huang's memoirs. But *Oscars so White* seems to have had only a modest effect. Perhaps the most humorous was #STARRINGJOHNCHO, a series of movie posters of recent Hollywood blockbusters like *The Martian* and *Spectre* with the Korean American actor John Cho's face photoshopped over the heads of leading Hollywood actors. The parody's mastermind, web designer William Yu, wanted to draw attention to the lack of Asian actors in lead male roles. While the attention was largely positive, few expect such antics to actually change Hollywood casting patterns very much. We cannot expect people, including self-professed white liberals or Asian Americans, to fully overcome the pervasive Western bias. Bankable Anglo-American actors like Matt Damon or Daniel Craig are not typecast by race. They can play heroes, villains, supporting roles, leading roles, Americans, Europeans, even nonwhite roles, all without much fuss.

In the 2016 Hollywood adaptation of the Marvel Comic, *Doctor Strange*, Scottish actress Tilda Swinton was chosen to play a character known as "the Ancient One", who happened to be a male Tibetan sorcerer in the original comic book. The producers of the movie presumably decided to change his sex and ethnicity to fit a more bankable star. Swinton also defended the decision pointing out Hollywood's laudable promotion of gender diversity. The Korean American comedian Margaret Cho responded that feminism doesn't excuse racism adding, "our stories are told by white actors over and over again and we feel at a loss to know how to cope with it."

Asian American actors are almost always cast to type. John Cho himself said, "being Asian American is part of who I am, not all of who I am." But in superficial Hollywood, image is what really counts. There, the image of the Asian is that of the perpetual foreigner, while the white man is the everyman. People everywhere accept this because there isn't a corner of the world where Anglo-American culture has not penetrated. But if history had taken a different turn back in the fifteenth century, we might be seeing a very different movie.

Whitey: A Screenplay

Setting: New Guandong, New China (the Chinese North American Empire), year 2500 AC (after Confucius).

Wang "Whitey" Smith is a 27 year-old English-New Chinese man-boy living with his adoptive Asian family in a leafy suburb of New Guandong. He was recently fired from his job at the local Golden Chopstick fast food restaurant. As a child, Wang was rescued from the East London ghetto of the Kongland province of the Chinese European Empire by a strict and childless New Chinese couple. His unwed teenage mother had apparently abandoned him during the last great uprising against Chinese colonial rule, which resulted in the creation of a militarized fence around Greater London.

The incoming Prime Minister of New China is a reactionary Asian nationalist (and former reality television host) who campaigned on a promise to restrict immigration from the European colonies, defend the "homeland" against real or suspected white terrorists, and deport millions of whites who live in New China illegally, all in an effort to "Make New China Great Again". He is also threatening war against Old China and its former European colonies over their unfair trade policies and the increasing dumping of white refugees. He wants to strengthen conservative Confucian values which he feels have been undermined by an effete liberal upper class too sympathetic to multiculturalism.

As a child, Wang was mercilessly bullied by Asian kids in school who would mock his appearance and tell him to "go back to stupid Kongland".

Once he was beat up by a Kung Fu gang who accused him of being a white terrorist. Whites make up 15% of the population. Some are descendants of early European immigrants or indentured servants who arrived on both shores of the New World in the wake of the first Chinese settlements five centuries before. Many are now well integrated into New Chinese society. But most whites, like Wang, are more recent economic or political refugees who arrived within the last half century. They are often in conflict with both poor "native Asians" as well as with other nonwhite immigrants. They are also looked down upon by both the old blood Europeans as well as by the New Chinese upper classes. Intermarriage between Asians and whites is fairly common, but Asian male/white female couples outnumber Asian female/white male couples three to one.

Racism against whites has become a more serious problem, largely fueled by the flood of refugees following the latest round of anti-colonial uprisings in Europe as well as the growth of social media with its viral videos of police brutality against young white men. While most upper class Asians are fairly tolerant, less educated native Asian working class men in rural areas have fueled the anti-white xenophobia culminating in the election of the current Prime Minister.

Asians dominate all the popular sports including table tennis, mixed martial arts, archery and team handball. Blacks, however, tend to beat them in track and make the best music. Jews and Asians win most of the Nobel Prizes. But what particularly bothers Wang are all those hit movies where the leading men are Asians who get to rescue a beautiful but helpless white girl from depraved white terrorists.

Wang had a crush on a Vietnamese girl who rejected him for a Chinese boy. He had another crush on a white immigrant girl who rejected him for a Korean boy. He rebelled against his strict fundamentalist Confucian parents, who never could come to terms with his refusal to "just become New Chinese". He drops out of school, has a few brushes with the law (getting arrested for disorderly conduct at a White Lives Matter demonstration, for example), and moves through a string of dead end jobs, most recently at that branch of the fast food franchise, Golden Chopstick. He is fired for getting into a fight with a drunk patron who taunts him to "go flip my golden dumpling, white boy!".

One day he impulsively decides to go back to his homeland in search of his roots. But once he lands at Kongland Airport, he is quickly disillusioned by the abject poverty and destitution that surrounds him and frustrated by his lack of fluency with English. The locals mock his uppity Chinese mannerisms and tell him to go back to New Guandong. At the base of the giant monument to General King Kong, the fifteenth century conqueror of England, he curses a world where white people are second-class citizens and Asians seem to dominate everything.

2

Race in the Face, Race on the Mind
Biology, Psychology, & Racial Stereotype

> Race is a social construct, not a scientific classification. In medicine, there is only one race: the human race.
>> The New England Journal of Medicine
>> May 3, 2001

> It is only at the first encounter that a face makes its full impression on us.
>> Arthur Schopenhauer

What is Race?

In a book dedicated to exploring the basis of racial stereotype, it is essential to pin down what we actually mean when we speak of *race*. According to Wikipedia, "race is a classification system used to categorize humans into large and distinct populations or groups by heritable phenotypic characteristics, geographic ancestry, physical appearance, and ethnicity." That's a bit vague. The Cambridge English Dictionary isn't any better. It defines race as "a group, especially of people, with particular similar physical characteristics, who are considered as belonging to the same type, or the fact of belonging to such a group" or "a group of people who share the same language, history, characteristics, etc." We are no closer to understanding what race really is, if anything at all.

The basic unit of biological classification is that of "species", defined as the set of related individuals that can and will generally interbreed in their natural habitat to produce fertile offspring. It's the only taxonomic level with a clear boundary. The same cannot be said of any of the levels above (genus, family, order, class, and phylum) or below (subspecies, race). All of those divisions are the result of human convention designed to subdivide naturally continuous differences into artificially distinct units.

Throughout the last century, the concept of race has been invoked in pursuit of invidious political agendas. Consequently, many otherwise sensible people prefer not to use the term at all. Even scientists like genome sequencing pioneer Craig Venter were quick to dismiss the very notion of discrete human races. But is race simply a social construct with no biological validity? Ask any child to sort out photographs of randomly chosen East Asian, Sub-Saharan African, and European visages, and you can bet the bank she'll do it perfectly. Is she just picking up on a social construct? I think not.

The Evolution of Race

To understand the biology of race, we need to go back to the dawn of the human race. Studies of genomic clustering have established that our species, *Homo sapiens sapiens*, evolved in Africa about 140,000 years ago. These humans were the descendants of a series of bipedal hominid species beginning with *Ardititthecus ramidus,* whose 5.5 million year old fossils were excavated in the Rift Valley of Ethiopia in 2001. Remarkably, our ancestors came out of Africa not once, but twice. In this sense, we are all Africans.

With the completion of the human genome project in 2001, evolutionary geneticists realized that certain specific DNA sequences could be useful in tracking the course of human evolution. The first is that of the *Y chromosome*. Only males carry a Y chromosome, and they pass it on intact to all of their sons, but to none of their daughters. Unlike other chromosomes, there is no shuffling of genes on the Y at conception. Thus a man's Y chromosome is a direct descendant of those in his paternal lineage. Aside from random mutations, its sequence remains identical from generation to generation.

The other special DNA is found inside mitochondria. These organelles are the descendants of ancient bacteria that were captured and harnessed inside what became the first eukaryotes over two billion years ago. Mitochondria have bits of genetic material left over from the days when they were free-living creatures, and this DNA, like that on the Y chromosome, does not participate in genetic recombination with the bulk of the parental genes. Everyone, male and female, has mitochondria inside their trillions of cells, and all of them are descendants of those in the original fertilized egg. Sperm contribute no mitochondria. Therefore, all mitochondrial DNA comes only from the maternal lineage. Aside from random mutations, mitochondrial DNA sequence is identical from generation to generation.

When geneticists compared Y chromosome and mitochondrial DNA from isolated human populations in many different parts of the world (a technique called *haplotype analysis*), they found similarities suggesting that all of these people had a single male and a single female ancestor who lived in Africa around 140,000 years ago. Let's call them African Adam and Eve. It is important to note that Adam and Eve were not the only people of their day. It's unlikely that they even lived at the same time. They probably shared the world with several thousand cousins. But the crucial fact is that it was their lineage alone that survived to the present day. All the mitochondrial and Y chromosome haplotypes of every human being alive now originated with African Adam and Eve, the other lineages having died out over the millennia.

The common origin of current haplotypes implies that humans passed through a population bottleneck 140,000 years ago. Perhaps a period of climate change or other natural calamity drastically reduced the human population to near extinction levels. Their numbers didn't rise significantly until the last great exodus out of Africa some 60,000 years later. It is at this point that human culture really took off. Cultural innovation gradually began to overtake biological evolution with the invention of language. But that doesn't mean that humans stopped evolving. Human genes and the traits they encode have been (and continue to be) subjected to intense selection pressure from our own cultural environment. Did brains evolve to host linguistic and cultural innovation, or did languages and cultures drive the evolution of the minds that created them? The answer to this chicken or egg riddle, like so much else in evolutionary biology, is probably a little of both.

At the time of the bottleneck, there was no geographic separation, and the human population was largely homogeneous. Everyone belonged to a single breeding pool. Because of different versions of genes (polymorphic alleles), individuals were distinctive in terms of physical appearance, personality, and so on, but those polymorphisms were randomly disseminated throughout the population. Geographic gradients in physical appearance had not yet emerged. Our ancestors were dark-skinned Africans, probably similar in appearance to modern day Bushmen, the world's oldest distinct ethnic group. But as people migrated out of Africa and ended up in isolated pockets in Australia, New Guinea, China, Europe, and the Americas, they carried with them particular assortments of genetic alleles that differed in proportion from those of the populations they left behind. This is known as the *founder effect*.

Founder populations were exposed to distinct selection pressures inherent in their new environments. For example, people living in northern latitudes were selected for pale skin, which is better penetrated by the sunlight necessary to convert vitamin D into its active form. Those who didn't have an allele conferring pale skin made less of the active form of vitamin D, absorbed less calcium through the gut, and consequently suffered from rickets, a debilitating disease of the bones that decreased their ability to bear children. Eventually dark-skinned people in Northern Europe died out and pale-skinned mutants took over. This is how Caucasians evolved. Present day Africans living in Norway or Nova Scotia do just fine because they get enough vitamin D through supplements in the modern diet.

Whole genome sequences have now been obtained from people around the world representing all the conventional races. The genetic differences are subtle. Africans, East Asians, and Caucasians cannot be distinguished on the basis of individual genes (all humans have the same genes). Nor do they generally have different versions of the same genes (with a few exceptions, all the allelic variations of each gene can be found in every race). The big difference comes from *allelic frequency* (the percentage of each allele of a particular gene in a given population). When we understand that races are simply clusters of genomic variation, the population distinctions come into focus. In a major statistical analysis published in the journal *Science*, geneticists Jun Li and Richard Myers analyzed over a thousand genomes from 51 populations [*Science, Feb 22, 2008*]. They were looking for significant clustering at over 650,000 sites of single nucleotide polymorphisms (SNPs) found in at least 1% of the population. The genomes were found to cluster into five major groups: Africans, East Asians, Caucasians, Australian aboriginals, and Native Americans. Moreover, the analysis was powerful enough to distinguish further subpopulations within each group, such as South Asians and North Africans. Contrary to modern political correctness, it appears that the classical taxonomy of racial variation is, in fact, largely supported by modern genetic data.

The Modern Denial of Race

So, does race exist? If one is referring to salient physical variants rooted in allelic frequencies amongst human populations separated geographically over the course of evolution, then the answer is yes. This is a better definition than the Wikipedia version. But there has been a vociferous denial of race amongst many social and even biological scientists over the last seventy years. The American Anthropological Association proclaims that "race is a recent human invention; [it] is about culture, not biology." Notable figures such as the evolutionary biologist Stephen Jay Gould, the physiologist Jared Diamond, and the population geneticist Richard Lewontin have all mounted assaults on biological basis of race. The modern day denial of race comes from two sources. The first is a reaction to the Nazi extermination camps of the Second World War, pithily summed up in the words of the influential Anglo-Jewish anthropologist Ashley Montagu: "the very word *race* is itself racist." In an effort to combat racism, many social scientists wanted to define race through the prism of history and culture, rather than grounding it in biology. They borrowed liberally from John Locke, Jean-Jacques Rousseau, and Karl Marx. Faced with the racist genocides of the twentieth century, the post-war intellectual tradition was blinded to scientific evidence. We can agree that racism and genocide are bad, but the job of science is not the job of ethics. On hindsight, much of the history of twentieth century social science can be summed up in one phrase: two wrongs do not make a right.

A second, and more subtle, assault on race comes from ideologically minded biologists like Lewontin who want to believe that gene-based racial differences are insignificant when compared to differences *within* races. The great population geneticist Sewall Wright came up with an equation that compares the average amount of genetic variation between individuals in two separate populations with the amount of variation between individuals within the same population: the *fixation index*. Humans have a fixation index of around 15%. This means that about 85% of the variation between people comes from genes that vary within a race, while only 15% of the variation comes from genes that vary between races. This was the crux of Lewontin's attack on the genetic significance of race. Moreover, those alleles that vary between populations are not randomly distributed, but follow geographical gradients. For example, gene variants for pale skin become less common as one travels from Norway to Africa, while those for dry earwax are more common in East Asia than in Europe. Because most genes assort independently of one another and because the allelic frequencies of these genes are often distributed geographically, racial variation is gradual and continuous. There are no sharp dividing lines between black, white, and Asian populations. Further eroding the fuzzy edges of race is the accelerating process of global intermarriage and the resulting increase in the number of interracial children. Consequently, biologists like Lewontin deny the argument that all human beings can be discretely lumped into three or five or seven races. Race is an arbitrary distinction.

But imagine a rainbow; just because red fades into yellow through orange doesn't imply that there are no individual colors. Similarly, the fuzzy boundaries of race don't imply that there are no separate races. As for the low fixation index, the fact remains that fifteen percent is not zero percent, and groups of blacks, whites, and Asians, despite all their individual distinctions and subgroup variations, are still largely distinguishable. Sewall Wright himself believed that a fixation index of 15% was significant enough to differentiate groups into subspecies. Furthermore, Lewontin missed the point that the 15% genetic difference between populations is not a random assortment of differences, but a correlated package of traits. This is referred to as "Lewontin's fallacy". Dark skin tends to correlate with bushy hair in African populations, pale skin tends to correlate with angular faces in European populations, and epicanthic eye folds tend to correlate with coarse straight hair in Asian populations. Fifteen percent may not sound like much, but the correlated package packs a salient punch of gestalt.

The Origins of Variation

The real question here is not whether race exists as a biological phenomenon (it does), but rather, what is the significance of racial variation in terms of biology and psychology? It has been a mere 80,000 years since the major human populations diverged from African Adam and Eve's common founder group. That's just a few ticks in the grand sweep of evolution; not enough time for much significant tinkering with the complex molecular machinery of life. Natural selection is a conservative process. Mutations build up randomly, but the vast majority of them are useless if not downright harmful for the individuals that inherit them, and so they get weeded out of the gene pool. Therefore, the genes responsible for important traits such as vision or language have been highly conserved over the course of racial diversification. The vast majority of genes that have been selected in the course of human evolution are likely to exhibit no racial variation. In this sense, the commonality of our species overshadows the diversity of our races.

Random founder effects and the natural selection of advantageous mutations may have driven the evolution of some polymorphic traits such as skin color, hair texture, and body habitus. They are also responsible for certain genetic diseases such as sickle cell anemia (which, in its milder heterozygous form, protects carriers from the malaria parasite endemic to African jungles) and cystic fibrosis (which, in its heterozygous form, offers some protection from the tuberculosis bacillus once common in northern Europe). But even more important than natural selection in shaping racial diversity is yet another concept introduced by Darwin: *sexual selection*.

It is believed that only ten percent of our DNA codes for genes. The other ninety percent is either "junk" or plays some role in the regulation of nearby genes. Additionally, a large proportion of the DNA in our genes lies in *introns* (non-coding regions) that are transcribed into messenger RNA, but not translated into protein. Finally much of the DNA that does get translated codes for non-essential parts of proteins. A point mutation in any of these areas (junk DNA, regulatory sequences, introns, or non-crucial coding regions) will only rarely result in any significant change of phenotype. Even when a germline mutation affects a protein's function, this may not affect the individual's chances of surviving long enough to sire viable offspring. Couple that with our highly evolved mutation repair systems and it's hard to see how racial differences could have been naturally selected in just 80,000 years. This is where sexual selection comes in. Even mutations with no direct effect on fitness may perceptibly alter an individual's appearance. Natural selection looks for differences that matter for survival, but sexual selection simply works on any differences that can be perceived.

Sexual selection may have been responsible for many of the apparently arbitrary physical variations seen throughout the world, such as the epicanthic (eyelid) fold found in most East Asians. It may have been selected by the first settlers in the Yangtze River Basin 40,000 years ago, when Asian women, for whatever reason, found it particularly attractive in the few Asian men who happened to have that mutation. So here's an attractive theory: some of those men also happened to be especially witty or sensitive or brave, and the shape of their eyes served as a useful marker for those other traits that co-segregated with it. Soon the descendants of these men outnumbered their round-eyed counterparts, allowing the genes producing the slanted-looking Oriental eye to become widespread throughout the East Asian population (a phenomenon known as *runaway selection*). Eventually, everyone within several thousand kilometers started to look Chinese. But that's a "just-so" story, which may not be true, and could never be proven anyway. More likely, the epicanthic fold was simply an arbitrary distinction salient enough to become the target of stereotype.

Richard Dawkins has another theory outlined in his book, *The Ancestor's Tale*. It is known that certain species of insects instinctively imprint on a particular plant on which they feed and lay their eggs. Occasionally, an individual makes a mistake and deposits her eggs on the wrong plant. The offspring subsequently fixates on this wrong plant, and mates with others who may have done the same. After many generations of imprinting, mating, and egg-laying on the wrong plant, her descendents become genetically isolated from the original population and are no longer willing or capable of breeding with the insects on the "right" plant. A speciation event has occurred. Something similar may have happened in the course of human history.

Primates are highly visual creatures with dedicated brain regions specialized to recognize the faces of their neighbors. They are also notoriously social creatures that live and breed in complex structured communities. It is likely that the two skills evolved in tandem. Face recognition enables monkeys to distinguish friend from foe, neighbor from stranger, cool kid from loser. Those endowed with genes that build more efficient neural circuits in their "face space" are more likely to select higher quality mates and sire offspring with superior face recognition software. They are also more proficient at climbing the social ladder. In the ensuing competition, the genes and circuits for improved socialization and visual discrimination spread throughout the population.

The invention (or evolution) of language took humans to a new level of cultural sophistication. Survival and mating success depended less and less on muscle and physical agility and more and more on the social skills. As we shall see later, much of this depends on the ability to understand other minds. But a significant amount depends on discriminating superficial physical features. Early communities may have been forged by the self-segregation of individuals based on small preexisting differences, facial features for example, which had already arisen through natural selection or random genetic drift. The human propensity to separate in-group from out-group combined with the power of culture further separated these populations through the invention of different languages, customs, and religions. These artificial boundaries were solidified through the subsequent emergence of moral emotions (to be discussed in chapter 4). People tended to mate with those who shared their tongues, values, faiths, and morals. They were discouraged from or even forbidden to marry those from outside those norms. These prohibitions eventually became genetic as well as cultural barriers to further intercourse regardless of geographic distance. The more two populations diverged culturally, the more isolated they became genetically, allowing the accumulation of more mutations coding for physical differences. And the more physically distinguishable two populations became, the more likely they were to become further isolated culturally. The spiral of meme-gene co-evolution has accelerated to this day.

Dawkins believes that a combination of sexual selection for externally visible features, allowing for the segregation social groups, and the cultural selection for social features, allowing for the segregation of breeding populations resulted in the emergence of distinct racial types characterized by an exaggeration of salient physical traits. Given enough time racial groups may even branch out into distinct species, as has happened to the many varieties of insects. But given the increasing globalization and intermarriage rates today, this is becoming less likely.

Is there more physical variation in humans than in other animal species? Interestingly, to our eyes, there seems to be very little obvious difference between two individual clown fish or emperor penguins or macaque monkeys. But perhaps the clown fish is better able to distinguish its own significant differences with one another. On a similar tack, do Chinese people really look more similar than white people, as many white people believe? Or do Caucasians look more similar to Chinese eyes? It seems to me that there really is more variation in the American and Western European population, but the heterogeneity is likely to be a historic effect of the last several centuries of European expansion. One would expect to see more racial variation in a cosmopolitan center like London or San Francisco.

The Origins of Stereotype

The ability to make quick judgments in the midst of uncertainty made a lot of survival sense over the 600 million years that complex animals have competed with one another for food and for sex. Nature can design creatures that take their time making certain that the rustle in the leaves is just the breeze and not a stealthy jaguar in wait. Those creatures ended up dead. It can design individuals who scrutinize every mole and blemish in an otherwise ideal mate. Those critics ended up single. The world is far too complex, the predators and prey too wily for any nervous system to model all possibilities accurately in real time. So nature comes up with creative shortcuts.

The brain's perceptual apparatus cannot represent everything, so it models contingencies through rough sketches that function to guide the output of the organism's motor systems. Completeness is sacrificed for simplicity, speed, and efficiency. This is evident from countless conditional learning experiments conducted on simple animals like sea slugs, fruit flies, and flatworms. When an organism repeatedly encounters a noxious stimulus, such as an electric shock, paired with a particular neutral odor like peppermint, it soon learns to associate peppermint with the shock. It makes no sense to wait and see if the shock is going to happen this time like it did last time; it's smarter to assume that it will, and anticipate accordingly. This sort of logical algorithm is literally built into the way synapses form. Nerve cells that discharge in synchrony (such as those that are stimulated by the scent of peppermint and those stimulated by the simultaneous electric shock) sprout more connections with each other than with other neurons that aren't active at the same time. To put it more simply, neurons that fire together, wire together. Neuroscientists call this phenomenon *Hebbian plasticity*.

Hebbian coincidence detection is the neural correlate of conditional learning. It is the process that allows an animal to *generalize*. In terms of neuroanatomy, Hebbian circuits connect visual and other sensory areas with the hippocampus, which is involved in memory storage, and with the amygdala, the generator of emotions. When an animal encounters a new stimulus, its brain immediately looks for a match from past experience and formulates an emotional response. Because the amygdala is also intimately connected to the hypothalamus-endocrine axis and to the autonomic/ visceral nervous systems, emotional responses are often experienced as "gut reactions". All of this happens very quickly and, in the case of humans, pre-consciously. This is not surprising given that the evolution of Hebbian circuits and conditional learning predates the emergence of consciousness by hundreds of millions of years.

The ability to generalize can easily be co-opted for use in choosing sexual partners based on superficial appearances. Animals cannot operate functional MRI scanners, serological assays, or DNA sequencers that could show how genetically fit a potential mate might prove to be. But they come equipped with apps that can work even better. The more brilliant a peacock's tail, the more intricate a warbler's song, the more curvy a woman's torso, the more likely it is that healthy offspring will result from sexual intercourse with those who possess them. Animals categorize potential mates by learning to recognize phenotypic markers that advertise general fitness. This leads to an interesting conclusion: just as the biology of Hebbian circuits has shaped the psychology of stereotype, the psychology of sexual selection has shaped the biology of physical appearance.

Simple animals like sea slugs are excellent generalizers. Birds and mammals drive the evolution of their bodies through sexual choice. Humans are capable of both, of course. But what sets us apart is our unique ability to think *symbolically*. An obvious example is the language instinct: a hardwired ability to parse the meaning of the world into arbitrary phonemes and syntax. It allows the brain to think in terms of metaphor and simile. Another is the neuroscience of social behavior. Humans categorize the social world so they can read other minds. Just as peahens are experts at judging biological fitness by analyzing the plumage of peacocks, humans are experts at interpersonal perspective-taking by analyzing the facial features of others. At best, this ability is a wonderful shortcut that enables us, at a glance, to assess what others may think or want without the need for language. At worst, it is the basis for prejudice and demonization.

There is a neural circuit for stereotype formation. Whenever you see something new, your brain triggers the Hebbian coincidence detector connecting the amygdala and the surrounding limbic system with your memory centers. If you had seen something similar in the past that was associated with something pleasurable or painful, then you will *feel an emotional reaction*. This is how the brain assigns *value*, positive or negative, to something or someone based on its similarity to prior experiences in our memory bank. We are obsessed by race because our perceptual machinery was designed to recognize superficial appearances and categorize them into neat mental cubbyholes. The subliminal association program is fast, effortless, and automatic, but it can be overridden by a slower, more effortful, and deliberate system.

Improving the First Impression

First impressions based on conditional learning are crucially important in how we assess other people, and this assessment often determines how we treat them. Experience and culture are good teachers with long track records, but they are not always right. Positive stereotypes can lead to unreasonable nepotism, just as negative stereotypes can invoke misplaced contempt and fear. Natural selection has hardwired the stereotype circuit into the brains of all animals. But fortunately, most humans are also born with anti-stereotype software that can help correct their biases. I will discuss three such programs: empathy, mentalizing, and reason.

One of the key breakthroughs in the last twenty years of neuroscience was the discovery of *mirror neurons.* These are neurons that fire not only when the subject moves her own hands or feels an emotion, but also when she observes another individual make a similar movement or express a similar emotion. Functional MRI (fMRI) and transcranial magnetic stimulation (TMS) studies suggest the existence of networks of mirror neurons scattered throughout both the sensory and motor cortex. One region especially rich in mirror properties is the *insula*, an island of cortex tucked deep in the lateral sulcus between the frontal and temporal lobes. The insula, especially on the right side, is active when subjects experience visceral pain, nausea, or disgust. It is also active when they imagine being in pain or thinking about something noxious. Finally, it is turned on when they watch others feeling pain or expressing a strong emotional reaction. Have you ever smiled back at a smiling stranger or winced when you saw someone stub her toe? The mirror properties of the insula may be the neural correlate of empathy. Those more capable of vicariously experiencing others' emotional states are less likely to stereotype them.

Another important concept in social neuroscience is *mentalizing*. It is the ability to figure out another person's intentions based on non-verbal cues. MIT cognitive scientist Rebecca Saxe has conducted experiments in which children were asked to decide who is more guilty: a person who kills a coworker by accidentally pouring cyanide (instead of sugar) into her coffee or the person who fails to poison a coworker by accidentally pouring sugar (instead of the intended cyanide) into the coffee. Four-year-old children tend to say the accidental poisoning is the more serious crime, while seven-year-olds (and most adults) believe that the failed *intent to harm* deserves more punishment. Interestingly, Saxe discovered that a small region of the brain near the right temporo-parietal junction (rTPJ) is necessary for making moral judgments based on another person's intentions. The rTPJ, which comes on line around five years of age, may be the center for understanding *intentionality*.

Empathizing and mentalizing may appear similar, but are actually two distinct processes. There are those who excel in one while being woefully deficient in the other. Sociopaths who brazenly swindle the elderly of their life savings are often master mindreaders who have no empathy for their victims. Individuals with high functioning autism can be quite empathetic, but lack the *theory of mind* necessary to understand the intentions of other people. Nonetheless, the two mechanisms do share the stage in cooperative behavior. Jamil Zaki and his colleagues at Harvard have discovered that the mirror regions associated with empathy are active when subjects passively view others cooperating in a business transaction. The mentalizing regions come on line when they are then instructed to describe the mental states of the actors. It appears that humans routinely deploy the empathizing and mentalizing modules together to offset possibly inaccurate stereotypes.

Finally, there is the human capacity for reason. It is clear that people automatically categorize strangers based on preconceived stereotypes of similar looking others. But what happens in the brain when those first impressions are updated upon closer inspection? Alexander Todorov, a psychologist at Princeton University, is interested in the neuroscience of first impressions. He has discovered that when people revise their initial assessments of others, there is increased activity in the *dorsolateral prefrontal cortex* (dPFC), the part of the brain responsible for working memory and cognitive control. Not only is this the largest and most recently evolved part of the human brain, it is also the last region to mature in neural development, only becoming fully functional in the third decade of life.

The PFC is where hard thinking is done, for example, calculating 17 x 27 in your head, memorizing a new phone number, learning a foreign language, or cooking a three course Thanksgiving dinner for the first time. It is the part of the brain you use when you need to concentrate, consciously block out distractions, or set aside a piece of information while working on a subroutine. In short, the PFC is the seat of reason. What is interesting is that the capacity of working memory is very limited; most people can only keep about six or seven random items of information (numbers or letters) on line for a minute or so while being otherwise engaged. In computer terms, it is a slow serial processor. Contrast that with the visual system or the amygdala or the insula, which are all very fast and efficient parallel processors.

The dual channel architecture of the human brain is unique in the animal kingdom. The more primitive automatic components that the psychologist Daniel Kahneman calls *System 1* are very good at making quick and dirty assessments under uncertainty and time pressure. But they are prone to generalization and subconscious bias. The more recently evolved, consciously controlled parts of the brain (*System 2)* are slow, cumbersome, and expensive. But they are rational. Being conscious creatures, we naturally believe that the entire mind is system 2, and delude ourselves into believing all our decisions are rational. But we are seriously mistaken. System 2 is but the brilliant tip of a giant iceberg submerged in the subconscious. *Most of our mental life is system 1.* Free will, self-identity, consciousness, and rationality are just illusions riding on its ever-shifting surface.

Yet we humans do possess consciousness and a capacity for rational analysis that, however feeble, gives us some veto power over our subconscious stereotype generators. As the neuroscientist Vilayanur Ramachandran once put it, "we may not have free will, but we do have free won't." Reason, along with our built-in empathy and mind-reading apps, allows us to counter inaccurate first impressions.

So to summarize, does race exist? Yes, but it's not very important. Does race matter? It shouldn't, but it does. For the rest of the book, I will direct these questions at what it means to be Asian in white America.

3

Chinks in the Library
Myths of Asian Intelligence

Chinese parents can order their kids to get straight A's. Western parents can only ask their kids to try their best. Chinese parents can say, "You're lazy. All your classmates are getting ahead of you." By contrast, Western parents have to struggle with their own conflicted feelings about achievement, and try to persuade themselves that they're not disappointed about how their kids turned out.

Amy Chua
Battle Hymn of the Tiger Mother

The best cure for discrimination…is more accurate and more extensive testing of mental abilities, because it would provide so much predictive information about an individual that no one would be tempted to factor in race or gender. (This, however, is an idea with no political future.)

Steven Pinker
The Blank Slate

Made in Taiwan

When I was an undergraduate at MIT in the late 1980's, there was a local joke that the initials of the school stood for "*Made in Taiwan*". In a place where roughly a third of the student body is Asian (Taiwanese or otherwise), one can take this as a backhanded compliment. In this chapter I will examine the nature and validity of the widespread claims of superior Asian intellect and its relation to academic achievement (the two are not the same). In so doing, I hope to explore the relative contributions of culture and heredity to the myth of Asian intelligence.

In the history of the Johns Hopkins *Study of Exceptional Talent* program designed to find mathematical prodigies, perhaps the two most remarkable individuals were a Chinese-American named Lenhard Ng, who scored a perfect 800 on the SAT math section at the age of ten, and a Chinese-Australian named Terence Tao, who came close with a score of 760 at age eight. Ng won gold medals at the International Mathematical Olympiad (IMO) starting at 15, graduated from Harvard University at 18 with degrees in mathematics and physics, followed up with a PhD in mathematics from MIT, and is now a professor at Duke University specializing in the differential topology of symplectic fields. As a child, his IQ was considered to be in the top one in a million for his age.

Terence Chi-Shen Tao was born in 1975 in Adelaide, South Australia to Chinese immigrant parents from Hong Kong. He was reportedly reading and doing simple arithmetic at age two, became the youngest IMO gold medalist at 13, published his first professional paper at 15, earned his doctorate in mathematics from Princeton by 20, became the youngest full professor in UCLA history at 24, and was one of the youngest recipients of the prestigious Fields Medal in 2006 for his contribution to the Green-Tao theorem on prime number progression.

Let me give you a few examples from my own experience. They include a particularly bright Korean girl in my sixth grade class who had been adopted by American parents. In my seventh grade class in a gritty public school in New Jersey, one of the top students was a boy whose father was an African-American GI who had met his Japanese wife while stationed in Okinawa. The valedictorian of my high school class was an Indian-American who scored 1540 (out of 1600) on his SAT, went on to graduate from Harvard University and Columbia Law School, and served as the U.S. Attorney for the Southern District of New York.

I was no mathematical prodigy like Ng or Tao, but I did well enough on my SAT's to get accepted to MIT. The smartest guy I met in my freshman class was a 16 year-old Chinese-American who triple majored in physics, electrical engineering, and computer science before graduating in three years. I think we both studied equally hard, but he was able to learn and retain more complex concepts than I ever could.

Asians and Asian Americans are overrepresented at all the top tier universities in the United States. As of 2010, Asian Americans comprised 4% of the U.S. population, but made up 15-25% of Ivy League undergraduates, and nearly a third of students at MIT, Cal Tech, and the top medical schools. These impressive numbers reflect how hard Asian students work to get into these schools. Perhaps the most extreme cases of Ivy League obsession come from South Korea.

Student life in South Korea is no picnic. Competition for the limited number of university slots is so fierce and cramming for the entrance exams so stressful that an alarming number of young people kill themselves every year. An outlet for those whose parents can afford it is the option of studying abroad. This is not the American version in which young people spend a semester drinking, partying, and trying to "find themselves" in youth hostels around the Mediterranean while ostensibly studying art history. In South Korea, academic success is the primary source of self-worth. So Korean parents are willing to pay top dollar to send their children to financially strapped American universities. The more prestigious the name brand, the better.

In an April 27, 2008 New York Times article, Sam Dillon reported that over 100,000 Korean students were studying in the United States, more than from any other foreign country except India and China. Korean undergraduates at Harvard make up the third largest foreign contingent after Canadians and Britons. The path is hard, but disciplined Koreans are up to the task. At the highly selective Daewon preparatory school outside Seoul, the average combined SAT score is 2203 out of 2400, over a hundred points ahead of Phillips Exeter Academy, one of the most prestigious private schools in the United States. Dillon described seventeen year-old Hyun Kyung Kim, who aced both the verbal and math sections of the SAT and was scheduled to take nine Advanced Placement tests in calculus, physics, chemistry, European history, and five other subjects that are not even taught at her academy, which she had taught herself from old textbooks in her spare time. Her fifteen-hour days cramming and memorizing French literature and English grammar left her no time to waste on dating, which was banned by her school anyway.

Asians and Asian Americans, along with Jews, consistently outperform other Americans in many scholastic endeavors including spelling and geography bees (usually dominated by children of Indian immigrants), science talent competitions (of the 40 finalists in the 2011 Intel Science Talent Search, 17 were of East Asian and 10 were of South Asian background), and, of course, the SATs. In the 2010 SAT, Asian Americans averaged 1636 out of 2400, whites averaged 1580, Hispanics averaged 1369, and African-Americans averaged 1277. How much of this achievement is due to hard work, parental pressure, and cultures that encourage respect for learning? How much of it is due to "innate intelligence", whatever that may mean? Environment, culture, and nature are important contributing factors that should be examined separately. Let's start with the Asian parenting style.

Amy Chua's memoir, *Battle Hymn of the Tiger Mother*, offers a candid and revealing look at the kind of home environment familiar to millions of Asian American children. Chua, a distinguished Chinese-American law professor at Yale, married to an equally distinguished Jewish law professor, writes about her strategy for molding her two young daughters into accomplished classical musicians. She sacrificed much of her energy and spare time on piano and violin lessons in an unrelenting quest for perfection that critics have described as borderline child abuse. She did this not because her daughters enjoyed it, but because Asian immigrant parents tend to equate their children's success with their own self-worth. The combination of great expectations and draconian discipline imposed on a child's mind usually does yield superior achievement. How happy or well adjusted that child will grow up to become, especially in Western society, is a more complex matter. Filial identity and respect for learning are cultural characteristics rooted deeply in Confucian philosophy, a topic we will explore in the next chapter.

Chua points out the stereotypical trajectory of Asian immigrant families: the first generation arrives with little more then the clothes on their backs, uncompromising ambition, and a stubborn willingness to sacrifice their own comfort for the dream that their children will one day achieve more than they could have hoped for themselves. The children of the second generation, in response, spend all their time in the library, scoring high grades and top college admissions while their classmates slack off. They earn the prestige and high paying jobs their parents couldn't manage. Finally, the children of the third generation are born into security and privilege, but as Chua says, "they will feel that they have individual rights guaranteed by the U.S. Constitution and therefore be much more likely to disobey their parents and ignore career advice." Humor aside, there is a lot of truth to this. Success, whether in school, sports, or business takes effort. All things being equal, an individual raised in a family and/or culture that emphasizes a strong work ethic is more likely to succeed than one who is not. But are things really equal? Can the Confucian work ethic and control-freak parents alone explain Asian academic success?

IQ, Success, and the "G Factor"

This is a good place to define "intelligence" and explore its relationship to both academic achievement and overall success in life. We all have an idea of what intelligence looks like, but those ideas are not all the same. Most of us would agree that common sense, analytical acumen, and memory are probably all important components, but what about hand-eye coordination or pitch recognition? Over a century ago, psychologists set out to create a battery of tests that could easily and reliably quantify intelligence in the general population. The results of their efforts include modern standard IQ tests such as the Stanford-Binet, the Wechsler Adult Intelligence Scale, and Raven's Progressive Matrices. These *psychometric* tests were designed to measure an individual's innate cognitive ability regardless of education, culture, or socio-economic background.

The subcomponents of IQ tests typically tap many different and seemingly unrelated skills including digit recall, vocabulary, calculation, spatial rotations, and reaction times. What's surprising is that for the majority of the population, these skills are highly correlated. With the occasional exception, people with good short-term memory also tend to react faster to stimuli; individuals who are good at math tend to have bigger vocabularies. These correlations are also found in SAT, GRE, MCAT, LSAT, and other aptitude tests commonly administered to students. The presence of correlations among seemingly disparate abilities point to a general cognitive capacity in the human brain. Psychologists call this capacity the *g factor*.

G is believed to account for about 50% of the variance in IQ and is relatively stable throughout the adult lifespan, barring dementia. Moreover, *g*, and intelligence in general, is highly heritable. If culture and family environment were the only determinants of a person's intelligence, then we would expect all children raised in similar circumstances to score equally well on SATs and IQ tests. Decades of research tell a different story. Identical twins separated soon after birth and raised in families of widely different culture, religion, and socio-economic background turn out surprisingly similar not only in personality and temperament, but also in scholastic aptitude and intelligence. On the other hand, adopted children score very differently on these measures from their unrelated siblings who were raised by the same parents in the same household and who attended the same schools. Identical twins (who share all of their genes) have an IQ concordance rate of around 80% regardless of whether they were raised together or in separate households. Non-identical siblings (who share an average of half their genes) raised in the same family have a concordance of around 50%. That rate drops to around 40% if the sibs are raised separately. Finally, biologically unrelated adoptive siblings have a 0% concordance rate. There is simply no doubt that genetics plays a huge role in intelligence.

But life is complicated. One should note that while IQ, which is largely hereditary, closely tracks standardized test scores, the fit is looser with academic success, and lesser still when predicting life success. It's true that kids with high IQs tend to get higher grades in school than those with low IQs. It's also true that better students are more likely to attend college, get higher paying jobs, and live in better neighborhoods, while poor students are more likely to drop out of school, be unemployed or end up incarcerated. But the correlation decreases as we move from general intelligence, which is largely determined by gene expression, to academic achievement, which is largely determined by motivation and culture, and professional success, which is largely determined by luck and hard work. Every one of these links involves complex interactions of genes and environment.

The neurological basis of g is still quite mysterious. What we do know is that it is highly heritable (80%) and largely unaffected by family environment. It manifests itself across many cognitive domains (memory, judgment, planning, motor dexterity, perceptual acuity, and creativity) starting in the first decade of life. This indicates that intelligence is a genetically determined property of connections within the developing brain, which permanently alters the efficiency, specificity, flexibility, and speed of cognitive processing. Intelligence isn't a simple gene-based trait like the color of Mendel's pea plants. Rather, it's likely to involve dozens or even hundreds of genes, whose expression patterns are modulated by complex, hierarchically organized regulatory networks. Many of these genes are likely to be involved in activity-dependent synaptic plasticity.

Computational geneticists and developmental neurobiologists are now harnessing the power of high throughput next generation DNA sequencers to try to solve the puzzle. One approach is to compare the genomes of "average people" (those whose IQs cluster around the mean, arbitrarily set at 100) with those three to four standard deviations above the mean (145 and above) and look for sequence differences that correlate with intelligence. This is the so-called *Genome Wide Association Study* or *GWAS* approach.

GWAS have been employed to look for the mutations responsible for many complex genetic disorders from autism and schizophrenia to breast cancer and leukemia. They are particularly useful at detecting genetic signals in disorders caused by a large number of relatively common mutations, each of which contributes a little bit to the disease. But they are not so good with diseases caused by a few very rare mutations, each of which is necessary and sufficient to cause the pathology. Many geneticists believe that a trait as important to human survival as intelligence is more likely to have evolved gradually through the accumulation of many beneficial alleles rather than suddenly through one or two "eureka" mutations. If so, then GWAS should be a reasonable approach to finding the genetic basis of intelligence. To this end, a group of scientists based in China is now collecting DNA samples from average and exceptionally intelligent cohorts (in both Asia and the United States) to run their GWAS. The success of these studies is predicated on the extent of *additive heredity*, the notion that the presence or absence of a particular allele in the genome confers a certain set amount of additional intelligence. It may well turn out, however, that it is the *regulation* of these genes, either through byzantine networks of cascading transcription factors or through epigenetic modification of proteins scaffolding the genes, that plays the leading role.

However GWAS turn out, it is clear that there is such a thing as innate intelligence, and that *within* any given population, it necessarily follows a normal (bell-shaped) distribution. Inside the bell curve, we can make valid individual comparisons. By definition, the tails will contain individuals who are naturally very bright or very dull, while most will cluster somewhere in the middle range straddling the 100 IQ inflection point. This is not controversial. But what can we say about intelligence comparisons *between* groups?

Race, Intelligence, and the Bell Curve

The mean IQ differences between races, while not zero, are modest (less than one standard deviation). However, because of the mathematical property of the bell curve, even a small mean difference translates to large differences at the tail. And it is an unfortunate fact of human psychology that extreme examples are exceptionally salient, especially when it comes to stereotypes. As a group, American blacks do have slightly lower mean IQs than whites, who, in turn, have lower mean IQs than Asians. This has fueled the ugly myth that most Asians are smart and most blacks are dull compared to most Caucasians.

For the vast majority of people of all races, this sort of ranking is senseless. There is just too much overlap between the groups to discern any significant distinction among them except at the very tail end of the curves. But because extreme cases like Terrence Tao get so much attention, there tends to be a perception bias. Daniel Kahneman calls the natural tendency to judge the probability of an event based on how easily an example comes to mind (rather than its actual probability) the *availability heuristic.*

Heuristics aside, the fact remains that the Asian bell curve really is shifted slightly to the right. How much of the right shift comes from nature and how much from nurture? Recall that at the individual level, 80% of intelligence is innate. Thus, given someone's genetic information, one can predict with 80% accuracy where he or she will lie on an intelligence curve. But this doesn't imply that 80% of the difference in intelligence *between* two groups is also genetically determined. Comparing groups and comparing the individuals within a group are two different things. The relative importance of the factors that contribute to the measure of individuals within a population may not be the same as those that contribute to the measure of the populations themselves. Groups sometimes have emergent properties that aggregate with mass. Specifically, the role of culture comes to mind.

Allow me to indulge you with an analogy from physics. Gravity is, quite mysteriously, by far the weakest fundamental force of nature. It is orders of magnitude weaker than the electromagnetic forces that, at the atomic and molecular level, give solid objects their property of hardness. Yet if we zoom out, gravity seems to be the stronger force: boulders roll down cliff-sides, planets orbit their stars, the Milky Way majestically pinwheels around its super-massive black hole. The discrepancy comes from the fact that attractive and repulsive electrostatic forces among positively and negatively charged atoms tend to cancel each other out while gravitational force simply increases with mass. So at the level of humans and stars, gravity is a much larger presence than electricity and magnetism. We can think of genes and culture in a similar way. The genetic variations that contribute to personality and intelligence play a large role at the individual level, but tend to cancel out when we look at population aggregates. Culture, by definition, is a collective property. We get a better feel for it as we examine more and more people. Culture grows with population, just as gravity grows with mass.

My feeling is that culture plays a much larger role in between-group IQ differences than within-group IQ differences. The Confucian value system that puts so much weight on learning and on respect for parents and teachers probably explains Asian kids' academic success more than any mean genetic advantage within their population. On the other hand, it seems premature to simply dismiss wholesale the possibility of a genetic component in between-group intelligence differences. Social psychologists have been grappling with this controversy for some time now.

The psychologists Arthur Jensen and J. Philippe Rushton support a *hereditarian model* in which the contributions of genes and environment to mean group intelligence are roughly 50/50. This theory has come under ferocious attack from mainstream social scientists who champion the *culture-only model*, which denies the very existence of innate group differences. Most of their adherents refuse to accept the hereditarian model not so much because it's bad science, but because they can't bring themselves to accept a conclusion shared by the perpetrators of slavery, genocide, and various forms of ethnic cleansing based on purported racial differences. But as I mentioned before, it is not the job of science to set a moral agenda.

The real question should be: can genetics at least partly explain the small (but not insignificant) IQ differences between races? All we can say at this time is that many comparative analyses conducted over the last half-century consistently support a 3-5 point IQ advantage in East Asians (living in Asia) compared with Caucasians and a modest SAT score advantage in Asian Americans compared with Caucasian Americans. The differences, while relatively modest, become much more salient at the extreme tail. In comparing groups, we can't do the type of identical twin studies that were so helpful in elucidating the role of heredity in individual intelligence. But we can look at something analogous: Asian American immigrants. Before we do that, let's examine another minority group to which Asian Americans are often compared.

Genes, Jews, and Geniuses

Jews make up roughly two percent of the American population and less than a quarter of one percent of the world population. Yet their influence in the arts and sciences is outsize. A quarter of Nobel Prize winners and Fields Medal recipients and half of the world's chess champions were of Jewish ancestry. They are overrepresented in medicine, law, academia, finance, and the Forbes 400 list of wealthiest Americans. And they are the only ethnic group to score higher on average than Asians on intelligence tests. So it's only natural that some of the questions we've been asking about Asian intelligence apply to Jewish intelligence as well.

The Ashkenazi Jews are an ancient people notable for several things.

First is their resilient cultural identity based on the rabbinical literary tradition (Jews were expected to read and interpret the Hebrew bible and its commentaries when most of their neighbors were illiterate). Second is the historically low rate of exogamy and in-conversion (those who marry out usually leave the Jewish fold and few gentiles convert). Third is their long history of persecution and segregation into middleman trades such as banking and commerce. Finally, there is the fact that they are susceptible to certain rare genetic disorders such as Tay-Sachs, which is caused by a metabolic defect that leads to lethal amounts of lipids deposited in the brain, and Bloom's Syndrome, which results from a mutation in a DNA repair enzyme leading to high rates of cancers. In a controversial 2006 paper in the Journal of Biosocial Science, Gregory Cochran, Jason Hardy, and Henry Harpending proposed that part of the explanation for superior Jewish intellect stems from selective pressure for the gene variants that enable quantitative and analytical thought. In the centuries when European Jews were barred from integrating into the general agrarian society, the most desirable occupations available involved living by one's wits. Over the dozens of generations in which the daughters of the most successful merchants married the sons of the most intellectual rabbis, selection for mutations in gene pathways enabling enhanced neural growth and proliferation became more common in the Jewish gene pool. Those with a single copy of those genes tended to develop brains and minds more likely to perform better on IQ tests and win Nobel Prizes, while those who inherited two copies unfortunately ended up with diseases like Tay-Sachs and Bloom's Syndrome. A good way to test the theory is to compare the IQs of individuals with one copy of these genes (heterozygotes) with those who have no copies.

The Cochran, Hardy, and Harpending hypothesis implies that other similarly isolated and inbred minority populations subject to intense selective pressure could also develop superior IQ. Can we apply this logic to the general Asian population, which shares the Jewish affinity for learning? Directed genetic selection can only lead to enhanced brain development in a relatively small minority that faces consistent social/ reproductive pressure for many generations. The Ashkenazi Jews of medieval Europe fit the bill nicely. Asians, on the other hand, are a large genetically heterogeneous population under no particular reproductive or social pressure compared to their neighbors. It would be highly surprising if Asian populations were found to have a preponderance of intelligence genes. But what about Asian Americans?

Asian Intelligence: Nature or Nurture?

Immigrants tend to be enterprising folks motivated to succeed against great odds. Unlike the Ashkenazim, Asian Americans are not an endogamous population subjected to the kind of multi-generational selective pressure that made the Jews more likely to carry the Tay-Sachs or Bloom's Syndrome genes. But they may have been self-selected in another way. The individuals who had the gumption to leave everything behind and start anew were more likely to have come from the right tail of the Asian intelligence curve to begin with. This "immigrant selection" results in a curious founder effect. The Asian immigrant class and their offspring would possess greater than average intelligence for both cultural and genetic reasons. What the Jews got through social discrimination, Asian Americans achieved through serendipitous self-selection.

This hypothesis can, in theory, be tested using the GWAS paradigm. One would start by collecting IQ scores and DNA from large standardized samples of Caucasians, Asians (in Asia), and Asian Americans. If we found no significant genetic differences among the three groups that track with their IQ differences, then we can assume that mean Asian (A) and Asian American (AA) IQ advantages over Caucasians (C) are simply due to an academically biased culture. On the other hand, if AA=A > C in terms of intelligence genes, then Asians and Asian Americans have both genetic and cultural advantages over whites. But if AA> A=C, then it is possible that Asian immigrants are a self-selected subgroup *within* the Asian population with a distinct genetic advantage over other Asians as well as a cultural advantage over Caucasians. Finally, if AA>A>C, then a complex multi-level hierarchy is possible with Asian immigrants on top both genetically (over both Asian Asians and whites) and culturally (over whites). We can test this further by comparing Asian Americans who grow up in Asian American families with those who were adopted by white families.

It is possible that groups with a genetic advantage in some area (intelligence, for example) may have a cultural advantage as well (respect for learning). This is not coincidental. Genes build neural circuits that enable behavior. Collective behavior creates culture. Cultural experience stimulates neural circuits that modify gene expression via activity dependent synaptic plasticity. The feedback loop of nature and nurture is well known to scientists. What is interesting is that, at least in terms of intelligence, the traffic seems to flow more from culture to genes than the other way around. Individuals living in a culture that happens to value intelligence compete sexually to select smarter mates, eventually increasing the frequency of intelligence-promoting alleles in the gene pool. But smart people are not necessarily more likely to mate with other smart people in cultures where intelligence is not valued.

Yogi Berra is reported to have said, "in theory, theory and practice are the same, but in practice, they're not." While the experiments I broadly outlined above sound straightforward in theory, they are likely to be very difficult to pull off in practice. First, given the wide variability of individuals in any population, the sample sizes required for meaningful results will need to be very large. But I suspect an even bigger problem comes from the moral sphere.

Those on the political left tend to be allergic to the notion of innate differences in intelligence, which have often been used to justify bad things like slavery and genocide. They cling to the idea that in order to preserve equal rights for minorities one must assume that all men (and women) were created equal. This is not what Thomas Jefferson meant when he penned the American Declaration of Independence. The evolutionary biologist Steven Jay Gould denied the very existence of inborn intelligence in his book, *The Mismeasure of Man*. Intentions aside, his argument is not only wrong, but also dangerous. It implies that the discovery of innate cognitive or psychological differences between groups of people necessarily opens the door for prejudice. The flip side is the assumption that people are all really the same in innate talent, temperament, and taste. Inequality must therefore be the result of bad society, not bad genes. To remedy inequality, well-meaning policy makers have enacted legislation that deliberately handicaps those who happen to be more intelligent or diligent. But imposing equality where there is none is as unfair as mistreating those who happen to be less fortunate.

It doesn't have to be this way. Morality and reality are not equivalent. *What is* is not the same as *what ought to be*.

The political philosopher John Rawls offers an alternative. In *A Theory of Justice*, he proposes the notion of a hypothetical social contract made under a "veil of ignorance". If people really did differ in innate abilities, which they do, and if one cannot choose or know which of those abilities one will get at birth, then a reasonable conception of justice would be a lottery that every veiled participant would willingly play. Rawls argues that the resulting contract would be a utilitarian one where the fortunate few are reasonably incentivized for the exercise of their talents, but the less well endowed are provided with a decent social safety net paid for by redistributive taxation. The morality of a society should be gauged not by how well it rewards its well off, but by how compassionately it cares for its downtrodden. The measurement of innate differences amongst individuals and groups is the role of psychology and biology. The precise calibration of the optimal tradeoff between freedom and equality based on those differences is the purpose of public policy. Science must seek truth but it should also inform morality.

It is possible that on average, Asians, in general, and Asian Americans, in particular, are more intelligent than Caucasians. If so, it would be for cultural reasons, but a genetic component cannot be ruled out. One should bear in mind that between-group differences are very small compared with individual differences within groups, but this is not necessarily true at the extreme right tail of the distribution curve. Regardless, no results of a particular study should inform how racial groups should be treated. Average differences are interesting, and they may explain why exceptional individuals cluster in certain groups, but all individuals deserve individual treatment.

4

The Bamboo Ceiling
The Reality of Asian Underachievement

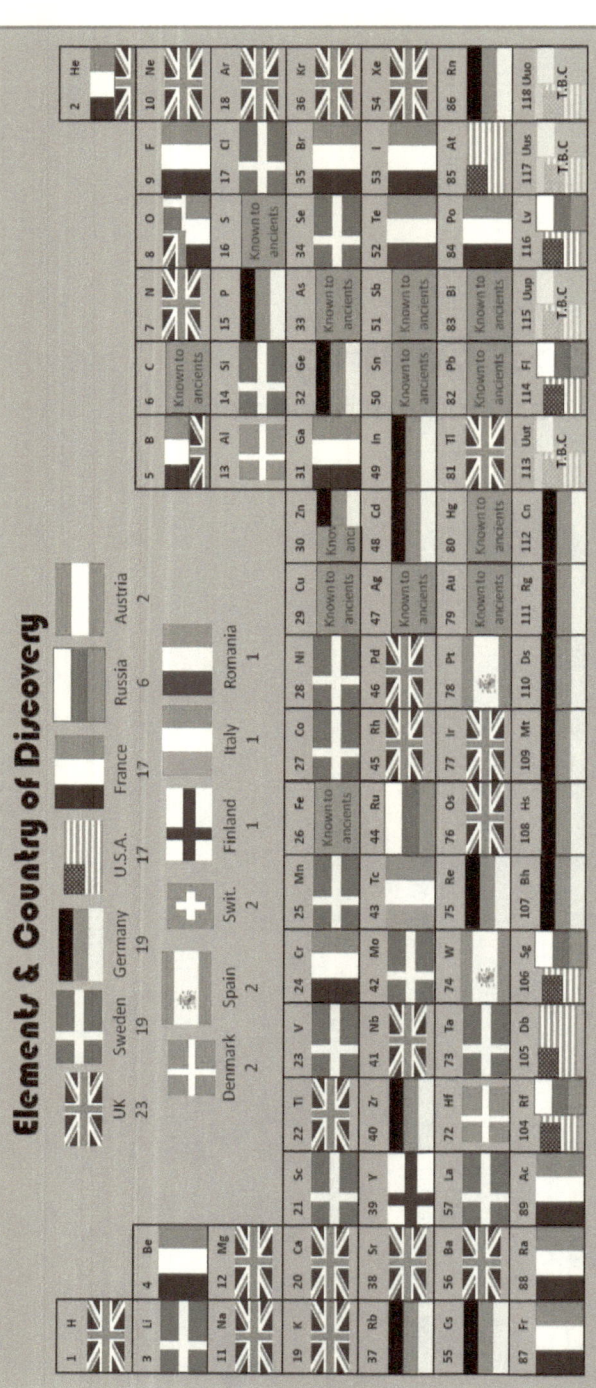

Elements & Country of Discovery

Collated by Jamie Gallagher, @jamiebgall

Credit given to both where joint or independently discovered. IUPAC recognised only.

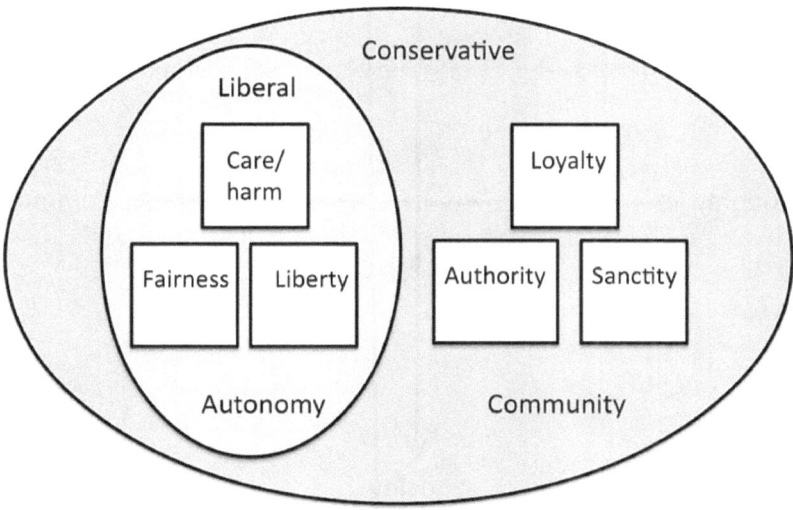

Figure 1

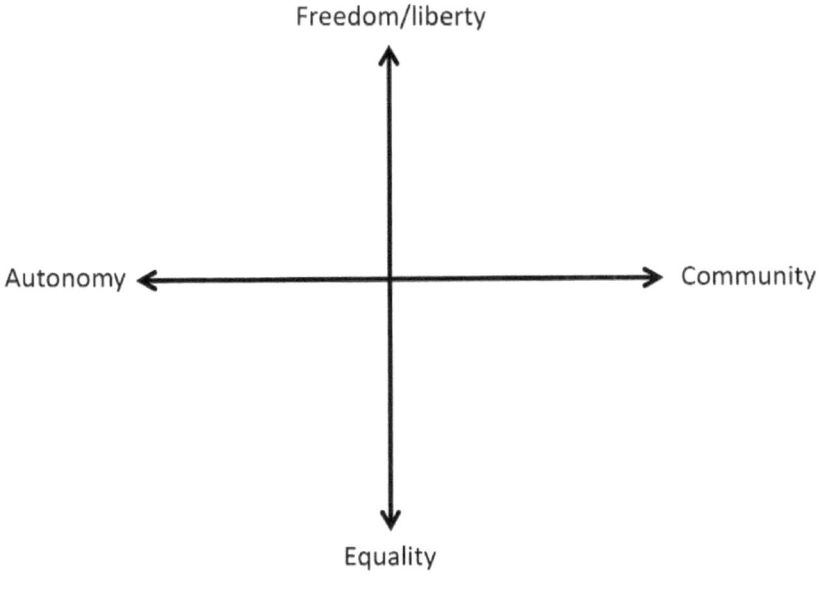

Figure 2

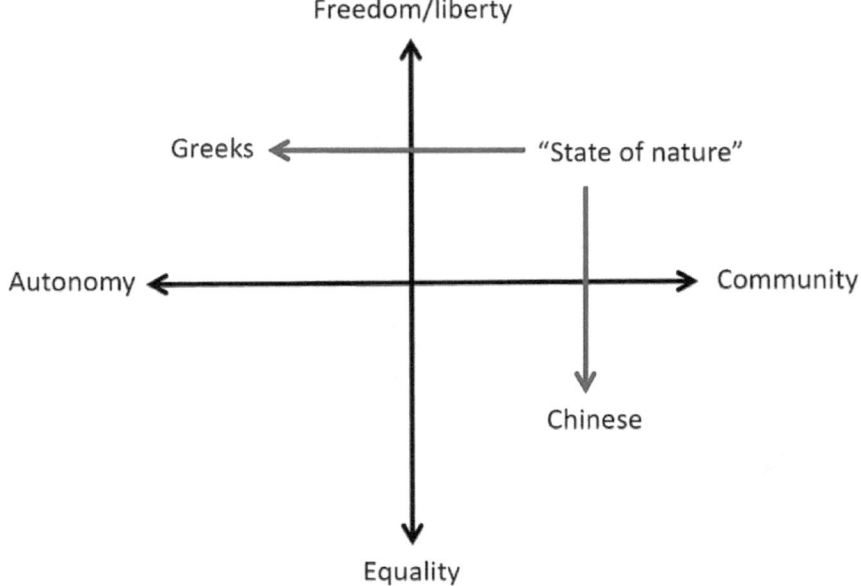

Figure 3

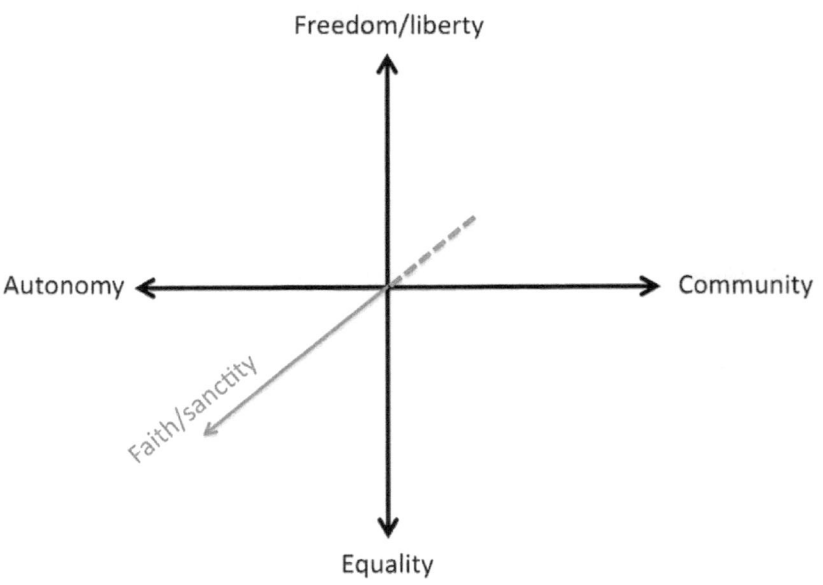

Figure 4

Those who in private life behave well towards their parents and elder brothers, in public life seldom show a disposition to resist the authority of their superiors.

Confucius, *Analects*

He who takes action fails.
He who grasps things loses them.
For this reason the sage takes no action and therefore does not fail.
He grasps nothing and therefore he does not lose anything.

Lao Tzu, *Tao-te Ching*

A century ago, Asians in America were feared as the "yellow peril." More recently they've been upgraded to "model minority". Less offensive perhaps, but still patronizing. Stereotypes have reasons. Asian Americans work harder, earn more, and save more than other ethnic groups. They're more disciplined and law abiding. They take family values to an extreme. They're so overrepresented at elite colleges that admission departments feel the need to discriminate against them. But are Asian Americans *really* that much more successful? Over the years, I've attended a fair number of academic conferences on topics ranging from biology to social psychology. What strikes me is the contrast between the large number of Asian faces in the crowd (undergraduates, graduate students, lab techs, post docs), with their relative scarcity at the podium.

Asian Americans are four percent of the U.S. population, 15 to 25 percent of undergraduates at the top universities, and almost a third of all medical students and scientific doctoral candidates. But it's downhill from there. Less than seven percent of science department heads at major universities, and only three percent of American Nobel Prize winners are Asian. Jews, by contrast, comprise two percent of the U.S. population. But they have won over a quarter of all Nobel Prizes in science (and half of those awarded in economics) since 1950. Nearly a quarter of *Forbes 400* companies have Jewish CEOs. In contrast, Asian Americans head less than one percent of major American companies. Most of the rest are WASP dominated. Author Jane Hyun, who coined the term "*bamboo ceiling*" in her book, *Breaking the Bamboo Ceiling: Career Strategies for Asians*, points out that "even in Silicon Valley, where Asian Americans comprise 30% of technology professionals, a study by the Pacific Studies Center found that Caucasians hold 80% of managerial positions versus 12.5% of Asian Americans." Is this discrimination in action? The answer isn't so simple.

Part of the problem is that a sizable proportion of Asian Americans are relatively recent immigrants who spent much of their time and effort grappling with a formidable language barrier while working overtime in laundries and groceries in the hopes of sending their kids to Harvard. Jewish immigrants a century ago faced similar hurdles. It takes a few generations to catch up. But that's where the similarity ends. Secular intellectual Jews are characteristically fiercely independent thinkers, whose courage and boldness are exemplified by the likes of Albert Einstein, Sydney Brenner, and Daniel Kahneman. They have the stuff that Nobel Prizes are made of. Asian Americans seem to be made of softer stuff.

And what of the great masses of Asians in the motherland? Postwar Japan has done well, and China's progress has been breathtaking, but these are recent developments. For most of the last 500 years, the West dominated the East. In the last century alone, much of Asia was torn apart by revolution, civil war, and imperial misadventures that killed tens of millions and stunted the development of every major nation on the continent. There is a Japanese saying: "the nail that sticks out gets hammered in." It's a lesson that East Asians and their immigrant progeny have learned too well over the centuries. In this chapter I will argue that for all their intelligence and diligence, native Asians and Asian Americans have been repeatedly hammered in their competition with Westerners not so much by external prejudice but by their own peculiar set of self-limiting character traits.

Interdependence

Asian employees are submissive, risk-averse, and lacking in creativity. They are quiet, passive, and uncritical. They make dependable grunts, but lousy managers. Generalizations like these have prompted employers to promote whites over equally or better-qualified Asian candidates. Often the discrimination is unintentional. But subconscious or not, the effect is the same. Asian applicants walk into the interview already wearing the Oriental stereotype like a scarlet letter. Worse, the cycle is self-perpetuating: as fewer Asians are hired or promoted, even otherwise fair-minded employers conclude that Asians perhaps weren't good enough to be there anyway, and the more Asian applicants themselves come to believe that they're probably unsuited for the job. Perception breeds reality. A record company agent reportedly told one aspiring Asian American singer that he had real talent, and that if he weren't Asian, he'd be signed. In order to thrive in corporate culture, Asian Americans need to be more assertive. Apparently, this is not a trait that comes naturally for many of them, hence the need for Hyun's how-to manual.

Are Asians really more passive and less creative than Westerners? In his book, *The Geography of Thought: How Asians and Westerners Think Differently...and Why*, psychologist Richard Nisbett details a remarkable series of comparative experiments conducted on Asian, Asian American, and Caucasian subjects. The results suggest that East Asians think about the world in fundamentally different ways from Westerners, which then leads to their differing patterns of behavior. The differences are deep. In the realms of perception and reasoning, Asians are more attuned to context while Westerners tend to focus more attention on objects in front of them. Easterners tend to think of the world as made up of continuous substances, while Westerners describe it in terms of discrete particles. Easterners believe the environment is continuously changing, unpredictable, and complex. Westerners believe it is static, predictable, and reducible. Westerners prefer to pigeonhole people and things into neat categories, while Easterners prefer to arrange them into informal relationships. Westerners are more likely to use logical arguments that are sometimes counterintuitive, while Easterners are more likely to use practical arguments that are not always logical. Easterners prefer compromise; Westerners prefer to win the argument.

Psychologist Herman Witkin developed a clever battery of tests to measure *field dependency*, the extent to which object perception is influenced by its surroundings. An example is the *Embedded Figures Test*, in which the participant is instructed to locate a simple shape hidden amongst a complex pattern. People who are good at this are said to be *field independent.* Interestingly, they include secular Jews (but not Orthodox Jews), high functioning autistics, and members of hunter-gatherer tribes (as opposed to farmers). People who are more distracted by the context are said to be *field dependent.* Asians are generally more field dependent than Westerners, while Asian Americans tend to be somewhere in between. It appears that the extent to which one's perceptions are framed by environment is directly proportional to one's level of socialization. People who live within a tight social matrix of family, religion, culture, political affiliation, and the like, also tend to perceive their world more holistically than those who are more isolated.

These distinct cognitive styles have had a deeply pervasive influence on the respective art, philosophy, and culture of East and West for thousands of years. It's obvious if you take a look at Chinese landscape paintings (like the one at the start of this chapter) or calligraphy. In Asian art, objects and figures aren't independent of one another; they "flow together". There are no discrete boundaries or sharp edges, just movement and transformation. What brought this about?

Geographic Determinism

A good starting point is Jared Diamond's influential book, *Guns, Germs, and Steel,* which explains modern cultural differences in terms of ecological constraints. Get a world globe (or a Google map) and take a close look at East Asia. The Chinese landmass sweeps a gentle semicircle into the Yellow Sea. At its northern periphery is the vast Gobi Desert. Its western edge is blocked by the Himalayas. There are only a few major islands (Hainan, Formosa, and the Japanese archipelago) and only one major peninsula (Korea) in the vicinity. China is cut by two long navigable rivers (the Hwang Ho and the Yangtze) and blessed with fertile valleys and a temperate climate. The geography supports two key historical observations. First, this land was made to reward hard working rice farmers. Second, it was relatively straightforward for one emperor to conquer and a single dynasty to maintain, often for hundreds of years.

Now spin the globe a quarter-turn clockwise. The European coastline is jagged. Rivers crisscross helter-skelter. Formidable mountain ranges separate innumerable alpine valleys. Eons of glaciation and the flooding of the Mediterranean basin have resulted in thousands of islands, peninsulas, bays, fiords, nooks, and crannies scattered willy-nilly. Climates vary from subtropical to arctic. This land was made to reward hard working fishermen, herders, and merchants. Europe was impossible to subjugate and unite for any length of time because the natives were always competing with one another for resources and novel means for attaining them. Charlemagne, Napoleon and Hitler could only hold on for a few years each; even the Roman Empire at its height never controlled more than half the continent. Unlike Chinese potentates, European rulers couldn't afford to become complacent once in power.

The ascendancy of modern European civilization was, simply put, the most important phenomenon in the last thousand years of human history. It poses a huge question that screams out for an answer. It wasn't always so. In the fifteenth century, a well-traveled thinker would have scoffed at the notion that descendants of benighted Europeans would one day forge societies that would eclipse all others on the planet. The Chinese seemed so much further ahead. In 1433, Admiral Zheng He circumnavigated the Indian Ocean and scouted the coast of Tanzania with a fleet of 317 ships and 28,000 sailors. This dwarfed Columbus's fleet sixty years later by a factor of a hundred. Twelfth century Hangzhou had a municipal population of over a million people who enjoyed public sanitation, irrigation, welfare, and recreation unknown in Europe. Their extensive canal system operated with pound locks; their boats were equipped with sternpost rudders and watertight compartments. They navigation kit included magnetic compasses. The Chinese invented dozens of different kinds of paper to be used for currency, painting, printing, and the toilet. Their astronomers systematically catalogued supernovae and measured the precession of the equinox. Their physicians developed homeopathic medicine and invented acupuncture. Their engineers invented stirrups, gunpowder, firecrackers, deep drilling, and the wheelbarrow. For a thousand years, the Chinese had the most advanced civilization on earth. What is remarkable isn't the fact that they failed, but how quickly the Europeans turned the table on them.

According to the British historian Niall Ferguson, the Western miracle was made possible by six key developments that the Asians did not invent: individualism, competition, the scientific method, market capitalism, democracy, and the Christian transmutation of work. Very broadly speaking, this explains European expansionism and the subsequent legacy of Asian collapse in its wake. For much of the rest of the chapter, I will explore each of these foundational factors, how they built on one another, and the reasons why white Europeans got them before the Asians. If we are to answer the question of Asian American underachievement, we must first understand this historic dynamic.

Let's start with perhaps the most fundamental difference between Asian and European culture: their differing conception of personal autonomy.

Harmony or Autonomy?

The crux of Diamond's argument is best stated in his own words: "geographic connectedness and only modest internal barriers gave China an initial advantage...But China's connectedness eventually became a disadvantage, because a decision by one despot could and repeatedly did halt innovation...As a result, in the very long run, technology may have developed most rapidly in regions with moderate connectedness, neither too high nor too low." Chinese civilization was an early success largely due to its geographic connectedness. But the unification process necessitated a significant sacrifice of freedom. In all societies, subjects trade some of their autonomy, willingly or otherwise, for security from the ruler/state apparatus. In China, this exchange was especially marked partly due to dynastic longevity, but perhaps more importantly as a result of rice cultivation, which requires more shared land than wheat farming or sheep herding. Many centuries of forced communal existence conditioned the Chinese to think of and treat one another in collectivistic terms. This puts a premium on harmony.

The playwright Arthur Miller once quipped, "the Chinese invented family. And they invented face." Richard Nisbett adds, "the Chinese were concerned less with issues of control of others or the environment than with self-control, so as to minimize friction with others in the family and village and make it easier to obey the requirements of the state. The ideal of happiness was not, as for the Greeks, a life allowing the free exercise of distinctive talents, but the satisfactions of a plain country life shared within a harmonious social network." In effect, East Asians domesticated themselves in response to the demands of a rice farming culture.

Diamond's ecological hypothesis of the East/West cultural divide is essentially correct, but I think it's incomplete. Geography and agriculture may have set the stage, but the real directors of the show were the philosophers, the prophets, and the potentates who then steered their respective societies over thousands of years. Oriental psychology had its roots in rice paddies, where it made survival sense to know your place and kow-tow to parents, teachers, and magistrates on risk of starvation. The ancient sages then formalized these subconscious attitudes and habits into Taoism, Buddhism, and Confucianism, and exported those practices to the rest of East and Southeast Asia, where they have now come to dominate the psychology of billions of people.

Historical context is crucial for understanding Asian psychology. Its difference with its European counterpart is cultural, not genetic. We know this because the children of Asian immigrants readily adopt Western attitudes. Moreover, the psychological changes can be highly plastic. A dramatic example comes from experiments conducted by the psychologists Kaiping Peng and Eric Knowles. Asian American subjects were shown a scene of fish swimming in a pond and later asked to describe the behavior of the fish. When the subjects were first *primed* by asking them to recall incidents that reminded them of their American identity, they described the disposition of the fish (their size, movement, intentions), but when they were primed by instances reminding them of their Asian identity, they spoke more of contextual factors (the flow of the water, the placement of the rocks and plants). Remarkably, independence and interdependency are culturally based cognitive biases with robust effects up to the level of basic perception.

Asians believe it's important to keep one's thoughts private, avoid conflict, and respect authority without hesitation. While many Westerners sympathize with such views, they tend to be more concerned about the rights and welfare of individuals, and about the pursuit of happiness and self-expression. The Western notions of autonomy and individualism are products of the Renaissance and the Enlightenment, but their roots extend further back to Ancient Greece.

Differing conceptions of freedom and individuality are central to the Oriental/Occidental divide. The Classical Greeks idealized a notion of personal agency during the centuries they spent as merchants at the crossroads of Eurasian trade routes. Their constant exposure to foreigners made them inquisitive. Their existential struggle against numerically superior Persians reinforced a sense of individualism. In the remarkable century and a half between the Persian Wars and the Alexandrian expansion, came the ideas of Plato and Aristotle. Platonic idealism and Aristotelian logic, in combination with rhetorical debate and mathematical proof (invented by Thales of Militus and Pythagoras, respectively), were the seeds for the Western exceptionalism that would germinate two thousand years later.

The Greeks invented Western Civilization 1.0, but they couldn't sustain it. The notion of man as free agent, boldly expressing himself through his creations and decisions, is an appealing illusion. "Freedom isn't free", according to a popular post 9-11 bumper sticker. It comes at the expense of the community that nurtures and protects the individuals within it. The ancient Chinese understood this. The Greeks loved their autonomy so much that they were unwilling and unable to unify themselves against the armies of Alexander the Great and then the Romans. And there was another fatal flaw. While the Greeks unleashed a remarkable burst of creativity in philosophy, art, and mathematics, they were hampered by a curious lack of empirical science.

It's not clear that failure was inevitable. The Platonic fixation with idealism was not an idea shared by all Greek thinkers, and it is certainly plausible that given another century or two, the heirs of Aristotle might have overcome their disdain for experimentation. If the Greek city-states had had more time and stability to let their ideas ferment, the human species might be colonizing the stars by now. But, alas, it was not to be. Western Civilization 2.0 would have to wait a further twenty centuries.

Confucius Say

Around the time Aristotle invented logic and Euclid proved geometry, Chinese sages were charting a different course. Forgive me for indulging in yet another useful analogy from physics: the wave/particle duality. People are not like particles following independent trajectories, they argued, but more like waves merging and dividing. The world is not neatly divisible into discrete categories, but is a fuzzy continuum in which everything affects everything else.

The elements of Chinese philosophy almost certainly predate the Zhou Dynasty awakening when the legendary sage Lao Tzu compiled his wisdom into the *I Ching*. Taoists drew attention to the natural processes of change they saw all around them: the diurnal cycle, the seasons, life, death, and rebirth. They believed in a spirit *"ch'I"* emerging from the interplay of opposites *"yin"* and *"yang"*, informing the way *"tao"* to live one's life. The implications of Taoism are simple yet profound: in a dynamic universe where the only certainty is uncertainty, the best policy is to accept what fate brings you, gracefully.

Confucius (551-479 BCE) is said to have been a close contemporary of Lao Tzu. His teachings, collected in the *Analects*, would become the cornerstone of East Asian ethics. Like the Taoists, the Confucians appreciated the need to embrace life's inevitable contradictions and uncertainties. But their focus was less on seeking harmony between man and nature, and more about finding the middle way among fellow human beings. Maintaining dignity and integrity within one's family and community should be the foremost purpose of life. The path comes from self-discipline, education, hard work, and the guidance of elders and ancestors, all traits in good supply among modern Asians.

The third great strand of thought to enter the Chinese psyche came from the further afield. The teachings of Gautama Buddha (563-483 BCE), yet another remarkable character of the Axial Age, were gradually imported from India across the Silk Road and over a period of centuries. The cultural exchange culminated in the epic journeys of a seventh century monk named Xuanzang, who crossed the Hindu Kush carrying sacred Buddhist scrolls to Chang'an (Xi'an), the great capital city of the Tang Dynasty, where they were translated into Chinese and readily incorporated into its rich philosophical tradition. It is somewhat ironic that Buddhism, an offshoot of Hinduism, had little lasting influence in the land of its birth. But one can understand why it exerted the kind of pull it did on medieval East Asians already well versed in the Analects and the I Ching. The central message of Buddhism is that one's life is a recurring episode in an endless series of struggles to reach *nirvana* (total unity with the cosmos), not unlike that of the Bill Murray character the movie, *Groundhog Day.* The pain of consciousness comes from the selfishness of being a self. Therefore, renouncing the self through meditation (or medication) is the path to enlightenment. Buddhism gives its adherents a compelling feeling of purpose amidst the seemingly pointless chain of existence. Passive resignation and self-denial may sound defeatist to more progressive sensibilities, but they resonated with the Chinese for two reasons. First, the notion of losing oneself complemented the Taoist goal of holistic integration. Secondly, denying selfish desires was instrumental in maintaining balance within both family and society. In many ways, Buddhism was able to bridge the disparate currents of Taoism and Confucianism.

Moral Foundations

Integration into community is a universal human characteristic. Hobbes was right to call life in the state of nature poor, nasty, brutish, and short. But he was wrong to call it solitary. Human nature is a product of natural selection. All creatures are engaged in a ceaseless struggle to reproduce themselves. It is a struggle in which the strongest individuals tend to survive. But humans and other primates have also evolved to be social. Fueled by testosterone, they stratify themselves in dominance hierarchies that influence mating patterns and resource allocation. Under the influence of oxytocin, they also form mutualistic kinships that cater to the young and the infirm. Finally, as we have seen, prehistoric humans developed hardwired brain circuits that allowed them to empathize with and understand others' mental states. These inborn traits form the basis of a universal moral sense that binds people across racial, ethnic, and cultural lines. Anthropologist Richard Shweder and social psychologist Jonathan Haidt have created a framework of "moral foundations" which they believe enabled our ancestors to suppress their selfish drives and made social life possible. [Figure 1]

Using their innate moral emotions as a guidepost, prehistoric hunter-gatherers created simple communities to pool their resources and promoted leaders who offered protection in return for tribute. These are reasonable trades. Haidt has said that he is glad there are places like New York City and San Francisco because the two coasts exemplify all that is technologically innovative and culturally enlightening about the United States. But if the entire country were made up of such cities, it would fall apart, because liberals are too selfish to commit the effort it takes to nurture large societies. Law and order, a strong military, devotion to family, respect for authority, and the belief in God make up the conservative core. Without them, there might never have been a prosperous nation from which great liberal cities could one day emerge. Conservatism and community go hand in hand, and were probably the default settings of early societies as they transitioned out of the state of nature.

Two Ways Out of Nature

Haidt believes that conservatives put equal weight on all five moral foundations, while liberals greatly emphasize fairness and harm/care over the others. This is why, historically speaking, conservatism has tended to be the more stable political system; it requires a strong leader to protect the community. But a serious danger of conservatism is the potential for tyranny, for it is as much in human nature to covet absolute power as it is to resist subjugation to it. There are two ways out of this trap: one comes from promoting fairness within the community. The other is a bold embrace of individualism. The Chinese took the first road. The Europeans tried both.

A useful way to think about this is to visualize a 2x2 grid plotting social autonomy against wealth distribution. [**Figure 2**] Let the horizontal axis represent the emphasis a culture puts on individualism/autonomy versus collectivism/community. Cultures on the right are more field dependent. Cultures on the left are more tolerant of self-expression.

The vertical axis represents a different concept: freedom versus equality in terms of resource allocation. It is an economic rather than a social gradient. People at the top are supporters of laissez-faire capitalism and minimalist government who believe it fair to sacrifice equality to the invisible hand of the free market. This is justified by the reality that human beings are not all equal in talent, temperament, or taste. Forcing artificial equality hurts the talented, the thrifty, and the tenacious. Those at the bottom are socialists who equate fairness with equality even if it means restraining those more willing and able. They also include Rawlsian liberals who believe it is important to level the playing field by taxing the well off to help the poor. This is justified by the assumption that although all people share an equal capacity for savoring pleasure and suffering pain, the relationship of happiness to wealth is not linear. Marginal losses at the top of a redistributive economy are outweighed by the resulting gain of utility at the bottom.

Life in the state of nature (i.e. Paleolithic times) was freer economically than it is today, because there was no taxation or monetary regulation. Law enforcement and the welfare system came from family and friends. The strong lorded it over the weak and disabled. But despite the economic freedom, people were less socially autonomous because individuals outside of the community were at the mercy of forces beyond their control, especially other people. The evolved social instinct is a survival mechanism that put prehistoric man squarely in the collective side of the graph. **[Figure 3]**

The ancient Chinese tackled the problem of tyranny by creating a socio-economic system rooted in the moral foundations of in-group loyalty and respect for authority, but diffused power down to the level of families rather than concentrating it at the top. They then added another moral foundation by sanctifying it in the quasi-religious amalgam of Confucianism, Taoism, and Buddhism. One could say that the Chinese invented compassionate conservatism by adding an egalitarian release valve to the right side of the graph, harmonizing authority within the community. This worked pretty well for two thousand years. The problem was that they ignored the individual dimension that would detonate Europe's cultural Big Bang. The Greeks, in the meantime, counteracted despotism by inventing individualism. This allowed them to move left, rather than down on the curve.

The meme of individualism inspired two centuries of continuous Greek achievement from Sappho to Socrates, Pindar to Plato, Aristophanes to Archimedes. But there were four reasons for their ultimate failure. First, the competitive field was too small to attain critical mass. Athens at its peak had a population of less than 20,000, and the total Greek-speaking population was probably not much more than a million. Second, their philosophy emphasized logic over empiricism. This precluded scientific and industrial revolutions. Third, they did not have a transformative religion that could have given their autonomy a sense of divine purpose. Finally, the Greeks were not united enough to defend themselves from invaders. In contrast, the Chinese were unified, but the cult of the collective was so stifling that individualism was never able to fully emerge from it.

In the interim, a group of radical Hebrews developed a novel vision of collective utopia that the Roman emperor Constantine would successfully export to the rest of Europe. Christianity reconciled fairness and empathy with loyalty and authority by appealing to sanctity, the last of the moral foundations. But it did not emphasize individualism. Early Christians instead preached self-denial, introversion, meditation, and submission. In this sense, Medieval Christianity was similar to Chinese philosophy. Western civilization 1.5 sank into a protracted torpor punctuated by periods of chaos and anarchy. But a later version of Christianity would prove to be an essential catalyst for the European explosion.

Between the collapse of the Western Roman Empire and the Italian Renaissance a thousand years later, China was far ahead of Europe in technology and wealth, largely because their government was more unified. The Confucian/Taoist/Buddhist value system that the Chinese exported to the rest of East and Southeast Asia balanced the authority of oriental despots with moral principles that were fair and empathetic within the context of community. So long as the harmony was maintained, and everyone knew his place in the system, society would prosper.

Now that we've tackled the Western conception of individualism, it's time to address Niall Ferguson's five other ingredients of the European miracle: competition, science, capitalism, democracy, and the Protestant work ethic. Together they created a social and political package that would eventually put Asians under a bamboo ceiling.

Competition

If you want to know who succeeded the ancient Greeks, go to the Cathedral of Santa Croce in Florence. Throughout the Middle Ages, this small city-state took a back seat to more powerful neighbors like Genoa, Venice, and Milan. But fueled by merchants and bankers backed by the powerful Medici clan, the city blossomed in the fifteenth century. Masaccio, Brunelleschi, and Machiavelli all walked her cobblestone streets. Florentine artists perfected the techniques of linear perspective, *sfumato,* and *chiaroscuro.* By the end of the century, Leonardo da Vinci and Michelangelo were working on Medici commissions. Not since Classical Athens, to which the Florentines consciously compared their city, was so much talent concentrated in one place.

Individualism had reentered the lexicon and Europe was ready to nurture it. The Black Death had weakened feudal conservatism by opening up new jobs and real estate. The Viking raiders were finally settling down on their plundered land. The population was beginning to rise. Once again, geographic and demographic factors were critical. The difference now was that life was even more competitive than it had been in Ancient Greece.

In fact, the competition became cutthroat. In the wake of the *reconquista*, the restless inhabitants of the Iberian Peninsula were stuck with a mass of unemployed conquistadors. But they were no longer looking for souls to save so much as riches to plunder. Serendipitously, a new outlet was opened up in uncharted waters by a pair of audacious Genoese. In 1492, Cristoforo Colombo, in the employ of the Kingdoms of Aragon and Castile, set sail out of Barcelona in search of India, but unwittingly made landfall in the Bahamas. Five years later, Giovanni Cabato, working for England's Henry VII, landed in Newfoundland while seeking the fabled Northwest Passage to China. Quite unwittingly, Spain and England laid claims to vast new playgrounds to fight over.

Not to be outdone, the Portuguese actually made it to India and China, and soon established control over an immense network of ports, forts, slave markets, and spice shops stretching from Angola to Goa, Macao to Makassar, the jungles of Amazonia to the deserts of Arabia. It is a testimony to the hubris of the time that in 1494 Pope Alexander VI drew a line around the globe dividing it between the Portuguese, who got the Eastern Hemisphere (Brazil, the Atlantic, the Middle East, Africa, India, China, and Indonesia), and the Spanish, who got the rest (everything from the Philippines to the Caribbean). Less then a century after Zheng He's journeys, the Portuguese had turned the Indian Ocean into their private lake. In a supreme case of historical irony, reactionary Ming princelings had ordered all their oceangoing ships and port facilities dismantled by this point, a fact many modern Chinese view with bitter regret.

Science and Industry

The Greek achievement, revolutionary as it was, turned out to be a double-edged sword. Platonic idealism introduced the dichotomy of subject and object. Its adherents divided the natural world into an abstract representation that they could think about and an external reality that they could see. Abstraction was useful for categorizing the world (into species or elements, for instance), and would later prove to be an essential tool for mathematicians and theoretical physicists. Although Plato was correct in believing that sensory perceptions are internal approximations of things out there, he downplayed their significance. But ignoring what you see limits the range of what you can think about. Later Greek thinkers, including Aristotle to some extent, were so enamored of Platonic models that they disdained empirical research. [The Romans who followed them were great practical engineers, but had remarkably little curiosity about the natural world; in this they were rather like the Chinese]. Without empiricism, there would be no scientific or industrial revolution in the ancient world.

The invention of the scientific method was instrumental to the rise of European power. The story of how it finally came together in the seventeenth century is a fascinating one. The Greeks started off on a promising path with Aristotelian logic and the progressive development of mathematics from Pythagoras to Euclid to Archimedes. But they were led astray by their failure to embrace evidence-based research. Pure logic and mathematics are useless unless applied to real world problems.

The Chinese were certainly clever, and they had a penchant for practical inventions. But they never embraced a logical and systematic approach to understanding their world. Rather, they were content to describe what they saw in terms of everyday life, and tinker with gadgets to make them useful for daily chores. In short, the Chinese were more pragmatic than idealistic, preferring concrete thinking to abstraction. They were also hampered by a Confucian conservatism that stressed moderation over radical innovation. Although a few individual scholars like the eleventh century geologist Shen Gua came close to independently discovering the scientific method, there was never enough of an academic environment to foster it. What was needed was a synthesis of Greek logic and Chinese empiricism.

This started to happen in late Medieval Europe. As early as the thirteenth century, people like Roger Bacon and William Ockham stressed the need for formulating hypotheses, conducting controlled experiments, and applying the principle of parsimony. This approach was finally brought to fruition by Galileo, who applied the logic of the scientific method to real world problems like the nature of falling bodies and the motion of heavenly bodies. The crowning achievement of Western science was undoubtedly Isaac Newton's *Philosophiae Naturalis Principia Mathematica*, which brought logic, mathematics (much of which Newton invented himself), and genius to bear on the natural world with astounding results. After that, things began to snowball.

Newton and his successors at the Royal Society legitimized and institutionalized the business of science through the circulation of peer-reviewed journals. More importantly, by assigning credit and awarding patents, they encouraged debate and competition that led to ever more discoveries and inventions. The competition was often as acrimonious as the debates were lively. Newton famously wrangled with Robert Hooke over the discovery of the inverse square law of gravitation, and with Gottfried Leibniz on priority in the fundamental theorem of calculus. But there was also cross-fertilization over generations and across fields. Within the Royal Society alone, Newton was just the brightest star amongst a constellation of brilliant luminaries including the astronomer Edmund Halley, the chemist Robert Boyle, the architect Christopher Wren, the mathematician John Wallis, the anatomist Thomas Willis, and the philosopher John Locke. The English corresponded regularly with their continental peers such as the Dutch mathematician-astronomer-physicist Christiaan Huygens, who was the instructor of Leibniz, who, in turn, taught calculus to the Swiss Bernoulli brothers, who later mentored Leonhard Euler, arguably the greatest mathematician of all time.

The best modern Asian scientists are as capable as any in the West because, as we have seen, intelligence is largely independent of culture and ethnicity. But the science they pursue is based on Western logic and methodology. The scientific method was a European invention exported to Asia only recently. It is no coincidence that most of the handful of ethnic Chinese Nobel Prize winners in the sciences did the bulk of their research in American and European labs, funded by Western institutions, and published in English language journals.

Market Capitalism

The late eighteenth century was characterized by three great revolutions. The first two were motivated by economic grievances in British North America and then in France. But the third and arguably most important one was fueled by consumer demand for cheap, mass-produced clothes. It happened in England, where the wool-based economy was ready for innovation and free markets were already being developed. It quickly spread to other industries in many other countries throughout Europe and the United States. Tinkerers like Richard Arkwright and Edmund Cartwright (inventors of the water frame and the steam-powered loom, respectively) quickly realized that improving the manufacturing efficiency of desirable goods, even by a tiny fraction, resulted in significant increases in profitability. The industrial revolution resulted from the practical application of James Watt's technical ingenuity to Adam Smith's free markets. The combination of individual freedom (to go shopping), competition (for profits), and scientific innovation started the road to Western domination.

The targets were the millions of consumers of industrially manufactured goods sold in markets all over the world. Entrepreneurs wanted their workers to make more stuff to sell, but only if they could get more consumers to buy the stuff. As the law of supply and demand would have it, expanding markets encouraged imperial expansion, both to exploit cheap workers and to appropriate raw materials. Rival empires also needed to defend themselves from one another, so there was pressure to invent better weapon systems and also to invade more territory in "self-defense". The major European mercantile powers may not have started off with the intention of taking over the world; they simply wanted to turn it into their own private supermarket. But that was exactly what happened in the arms race that ensued. There is some truth to the saying that the British acquired their empire in a fit of absence of mind.

Asians are no strangers to capitalism, as evident from their countless teeming bazaars. Without an emphasis on individual autonomy, however, there can be no great demand for nonessential goods. And without scientific innovation, there can be no industry to mass-produce them. Market capitalism in Asia never achieved the scale it did in the West until the late twentieth century, when American-style economic policies were finally fully adopted and implemented. By then, Asian capitalism was simply Western capitalism with an Eastern face.

Democracy

The symbiotic relationship between energy and information is a strangely recurring theme throughout the sciences from physics to biochemistry to neuroscience. Market capitalism and the military-industrial complex powered Western success, and the ideas of liberal democracy followed soon after. Or perhaps it was it the other way around. The First Amendment freedoms that Americans take for granted: those of speech, press, and assembly, have a long and arduous history dating back to centuries of feuds between monarchs and barons in medieval England. By the latter part of the seventeenth century, after the ordeal of regicide and civil war, there were two opposing schools of political philosophy. Thomas Hobbes sided with the sovereign, provided that he was enlightened enough to protect his subjects from themselves. His *Leviathan* was an allegory for a harmonious collective, not unlike Confucian China, presided over by a benevolent emperor who embodied the spirit of his constituents. And as in Confucian China, the integrity of the state takes precedence over the will of individuals.

John Locke was of a different mind. In his *Second Treatise of Government*, he formulated the notion of society as a social contract between independent contractors who negotiate a transfer of power for their mutual benefit. There are no divine rights or collective agencies involved, just free individuals making rational decisions. Implicit in Locke's philosophy is the assumption that no ruler or potentate has any legitimate power over another. Locke believed the state should exist to protect its citizens, not the reverse.

With the ouster of King James II in the so-called Glorious Revolution of 1688, Locke's side won out. England would thereafter be governed by a succession of rubber-stamp monarchs beholden to the will of the people as expressed through their representatives in Parliament. Freedom of self-expression, invented by the Greeks, had become institutionalized through liberal democracy. Locke's vision of government would serve as the inspiration for Thomas Jefferson's *Declaration of Independence* (1776), and become the foundation of modern liberalism. But it was the genius of the English people to realize that liberalism must be defended by conservative foundations.

Edmund Burke, Hobbes' intellectual descendant and the father of modern conservatism, provided one foundation by appealing to the wisdom of tradition and culture. Adam Smith's free market was another. Finally, the power of the Royal Navy in defense of the realm cannot be overlooked. With their conservative institutions, the Anglo-Saxons had imbued the liberal idea with tremendous energy.

There is a fundamental difference between traditional East Asian and modern Western European political philosophy. In Western democracies, the right and the left offer different ways of protecting individual rights; the former emphasizes free enterprise while the latter stresses social fairness. But both generally view the state in Lockean terms: it is a means to protect and expand the welfare of individuals. In stark contrast, Asian society is grounded in the Hobbsian notion of the state as an organic entity that justifies its own existence.

The Protestant Work Ethic

In his remarkable book, *Human Accomplishment*, Charles Murray writes of Europe, "despite its small size, common Christian heritage, and common racial heritage, a few places in Europe have been home to far more intense levels of human accomplishment than other places... the numbers of significant figures from Britain, France, and Germany dwarf those from everywhere else except Italy." Murray's analysis of the distribution of great achievement in the arts and sciences over the last 500 years makes three interesting points. First, within the geographic core bordered by England, eastern France, northern Italy, and Germany, most of the brightest stars made their marks in cosmopolitan centers like London, Paris, and Amsterdam. Second, there is a historic shift in the achievement pattern from Catholic south (notably northern Italy) to Protestant north (especially Germany and England) in the seventeenth century. Third, Western success came largely from two demographics: Renaissance Catholics followed by post-Reformation Protestants.

The historian Samuel Huntington defines contemporary "Western Civilization" as follows: North America north of Mexico, Australia and New Zealand, and Western Europe (west of Poland). He excludes all of Africa, Latin America, the Middle East (including Israel), Asia, Greece, and Russia. What is left is basically Murray's European core plus the white Anglo-Saxon colonies (the so-called Anglosphere). The lion's share of the world's wealth, military might, political influence, scientific and technological innovations, and artistic achievements over the last 400 years have come from here. From Shakespeare to Shelley, Bach to the Beatles, Gauss to Google, the West really has been the best. Paradoxically, religion played a crucial role in kick-starting the process.

Recall that sanctity is one of Jonathan Haidt's five moral foundations. Haidt and the psychologist Paul Rozin have discovered that at the root of sanctity lies the emotion of *disgust*. Disgust is a universal human trait that evolved to protect us from infection. Substances that harbor disease-causing microorganisms, such as feces and decaying flesh, and their associated odors produce a natural revulsion characterized by a distinctive and unmistakable facial expression often accompanied by a gag reflex. This emotional response was adaptive for omnivorous apes that faced dining options that often came with black box warnings. Those equipped with an instinctive autonomic alarm system set to go off at the sight or smell of potential disease-causing vectors had a selective survival advantage. Like many other domains of the brain, the disgust module is deployed automatically, but the emotion eventually reaches the cerebral cortex where it becomes a conscious feeling that can be taken over by the rational system and used for purposes other than those for which it was initially selected.

Disgust is not only a useful response to dangerous foods, but can be extended to the other moral foundations as well. As our ancestors began to live in larger communities, there was an advantage to sharing common values and suppressing selfish desires. The emotion of disgust gave rise to its mirror opposite, sanctity, and the two were then co-opted to help reinforce the moral emotions that people already possessed: fairness, empathy, community, and authority. Shared disgust (such as food taboos) and shared respect for common goals and good deeds acquired a religious aura that strengthened group bonds. Sanctity (or purity) is a tool that our minds have fashioned out of the emotion of disgust to suppress selfishness and promote social cohesion. All political persuasions use the foundation of sanctity. Liberals deploy it to bolster fairness and empathy, while conservatives use it to buttress community and authority.

So sanctity serves two functions. Many things considered taboo, such as consumption of raw shellfish or incestuous intercourse, can have real detrimental consequences such as gastroenteritis or congenital birth defects. But quite separate from that, sacred things often serve to bind communities together. Communities establish taboos by co-opting the natural instinct of disgust, and they sanctify things by co-opting the natural capacity for religiosity.

The objects of sanctity and taboo need not be rooted in anything physiological. But because sanctimonious emotion itself comes from subconscious brain circuits, it gives those targets a sense of conviction more powerful than reason can allow. In secular societies, people may be bound to an occupation by a sense of obligation, but religion elevates it to the level of a "calling". It has been said that an occupation is something you do to get paid, but a calling is something you would willingly pay to do. The faith that comes from sanctity is quite distinct from social and economic autonomy. We can add the dimension of sanctity/faith to our graph of moral space. [figure 4]

The Chinese and the Romans both recruited religion to strengthen their empires. In its original inception, Christianity strongly encouraged sacrifice in preparation for the afterlife. Influenced by Plato, the early Christians rejected the physical world and its attendant bodily sensations. In this, they were no more supportive of autonomy than the ancient Chinese. But Christianity would gradually take a different turn in Western Europe.

Thanks to the same geographical and economic factors responsible for the rise of Classical Greece seventeen centuries before, the moribund thinking of the Middle Ages eventually began to thaw. In the thirteenth century, Thomas Aquinas grafted humanism and its emphasis on individual autonomy onto Christian theology. In essence, he preached that men should think of themselves as reflections of a more perfect God while still living and acting as free agents in the material world. Creative geniuses like Michelangelo and Leonardo heeded the call. Under the auspices of the Catholic Church, Classicism made a comeback. A handful of artists of renown and their elite patrons throughout the Italian city-states embraced this first explosion of Christian humanism. But it wasn't something readily accessible to the masses of common folk tethered to the conservative habits of their ancestral traditions. What was needed was a more radical reformation from the bottom-up.

The next stage of Christian transmutation happened in Germany and Switzerland in the early sixteenth century. A mass of disenchanted Catholics alienated by the corruption and cynicism of the times (epitomized by Pope Julius Medici's sale of indulgences to gullible peasants guaranteeing them time off from Purgatory) yearned for a more direct approach to God. Critically, those who felt most excluded by the Catholic Church also tended to be the most thrifty and industrious. They threw their support behind Martin Luther and John Calvin. Lutheranism and Calvinism had natural appeal to a middle class rising throughout northern Europe. Their emphasis on close study of the scriptures, recently made possible by Gutenberg's printing press, had a positive effect on literacy and education. Their stress on fiscal prudence furthered commerce and capitalism. Their struggles for acceptance as minority religions encouraged their followers to embrace the ideals of democracy. And their encouragement of free thought stimulated scientific inquiry. The ingredients of the Western miracle further fermented.

The Protestant Reformation sanctified hard work and thrift in the name of godliness. Remarkably, this sanctification persisted even as European society became more secular and as the belief in God itself become secondary. What mattered now was one's self-confidence in the pursuit of worldly achievements. Individualism grounded in the power of faith allowed the common folk of northern Europe to pursue whatever interested them not as idle hobbies, or even as necessary jobs, but as higher callings.

Luther and Calvin didn't see themselves as liberals. Many of their followers were ignorant bigots who routinely tortured and burned nonbelievers (often other Protestants) at the stake. But in their quest to become better Christians, they unwittingly unleashed an economic dynamism that would propel Western civilization and its increasingly liberal ideas to their zenith. Nowhere was this process more dramatic than in Great Britain.

By the mid nineteenth century, British society had become a well-oiled machine. English culture and ideas, inspired by the Protestant work ethic, legislated through parliamentary debate, powered by Victorian industry, exchanged in free markets, and defended by gunships of the Royal Navy began to dominate the globe. The quest to satisfy market demand got them into trouble in Boston, where rebellious colonists refused to buy Indian tea, and in Beijing, where conscientious administrators refused to buy Indian opium. The British jettisoned their Americans, but got even richer trading with them. They won the Opium Wars with gunboats up the Yangtze. In a remarkable turn of events, the West had triumphed by grounding progressive liberalism in conservative institutions. From Shanghai to Singapore, a bamboo ceiling had descended over the heads of a billion Asians.

Communist Catastrophe

The advent of Western industrialization in the nineteenth century generated unprecedented wealth for the ruling classes and unprecedented urban poverty for the working classes. Popular discontent, always simmering under the surface, periodically boiled over into armed insurrection and occasional revolution, most notably in 1848. Conservative governments responded with military crackdowns, with mixed success. Liberal governments did much the same, combined with some promises of reform and modest franchise expansion, most notably in Britain in 1832. Against this background came the radical ideas of Karl Marx and Freidrich Engels, outlined in *The Communist Manifesto*.

Marx and Engels predicted a worldwide communist revolution whose epicenter would be Western Europe, where income inequality was highest and industrialization most dehumanizing. It never happened. Massive poverty continued to plague the industrialized states, but generally speaking, the conditions of the working classes did gradually improve over the next two centuries thanks to spreading democracy, responsible government, and public health measures. Where communism did succeed was in the more backward states to the east. It is ironic that while none of the great cultural innovations that made modern Europe so dominant (individualism, competition, science, capitalism, democracy, the Protestant work ethic) were readily adopted by the Asians, the one invention which was (communism), just happened to be the one voted most likely to fail.

The last days of the Qing Dynasty were marked by widespread social chaos and economic collapse. Warlords and foreign armies roamed the countryside. The rulers were hopelessly corrupt and out of touch. Reformers could choose to cooperate with the Western democracies and sell their nation into subservience, or they could take the other path towards socialist self-sufficiency. Mao Zedong, a charismatic child of simple peasants, had grandiose dreams. In the 1930's, he witnessed Stalin's brutally effective collectivization and breakneck industrialization first hand. He realized how easily the Soviet system could be molded to fit the Chinese mentality. In 1949, after decades of long marches and guerrilla warfare, Chairman Mao defeated his Nationalist rivals and was ready to begin his grand experiment.

Mao successfully kept the Chinese Communist party together during the uncertain years following the revolution. His poems and proverbs, collected in the "Little Red Book", became the bible of a half a billion hungry souls seeking a sense of direction in a world turned upside down. Like Stalin, he carefully cultivated a cult of personality, and cemented it with an active ministry of propaganda, an official policy of disinformation, and ruthless purges of questionable party members. Furthermore, he was able to capitalize on the ancient Chinese legacy of emperor worship. It is more apt to describe Mao not as a new communist emperor, but rather, as a new emperor who happened to pay lip service to communism.

The first decade of Mao's reign was marked by radical social re-engineering along the lines of Soviet central planning committees, but on an even grander scale. Millions of private farms were collectivized, families were torn asunder, and those found suspect were shot or imprisoned in remote re-education camps, often for decades. Then came the ironically named "Great Leap Forward" in 1957. This was just the first of Mao's gargantuan failures. Mao replaced a culture richly grounded in three thousand years of family values with his own perverted personality cult inspired by a pair of German philosophers (Marx and Engels) and modeled on the modus operandi of a pair of Russian thugs (Lenin and Stalin). The result was a catastrophe of incomprehensible magnitude.

In an effort to boost economic development, the communists imposed strict quotas on productivity and enforced them through corporal punishment. Peasants were forced off their farms and ordered to smelt steel in their backyards. Overzealous party officials exaggerated productivity figures, while the state monopoly stifled incentive. The top-down approach was a deathblow to private enterprise. Shoddy goods flooded the market, while essentials fell by the wayside. The moderating influence of the family unit, the very backbone of Chinese civilization, disintegrated. Between 1958 and 1962, an estimated *thirty million* people perished in the worst famine of all time. The desperate resorted to cannibalism. Throughout it all (and even to this day), the Chinese leadership was unable or unwilling to acknowledge its murderous blunder.

The Chairman's later years were characterized by a progressive descent into megalomania. The Cultural Revolution of the late 1960s coincided with the rock and roll-fueled countercultural demonstrations bursting out from London and Los Angeles to Paris and Prague. And like the others, it was driven by armies of disaffected youth. This is where the similarity ends. The fanatical Red Guards were students and teenagers motivated by an irrational attachment to Mao's revolutionary teachings. They didn't want a world of peace, love, and understanding; they wanted a world of Mao. But if you go carrying pictures of Chairman Mao, you ain't gonna make it with anyone anyhow. The Chairman unleashed his mobs on the enterprising, the ambitious, the educated, the moderates, and, eventually, anyone of social stature or economic means, in a misguided attempt to rekindle the revolutionary spirit of his own youth. In the West, the hippies were radicalizing liberalism. In China, the Red Guards were radicalizing despotism. It was a time neither of autonomy nor of faith.

Over a million people were killed outright by vicious thugs well versed in the martial arts. Several million more were shipped off to hard labor camps for "re-education", including the elderly Pu Yi, the Qing Dynasty's hapless last emperor. The son of Deng Xiaoping, who would later become Chairman of the Communist Party, was permanently maimed by Kung-fu fighting hooligans. Instead of revitalizing Chinese society, as Mao had hoped, the Cultural Revolution set it back at least a generation. In 1913, the average American was ten times wealthier than his Chinese counterpart. By 1968, the gap had widened to a factor of thirty-three and continued to increase at least until the mid seventies. Today Mao's visage is still on display on giant posters in the middle of Tiananmen Square. The Chinese downloaded the wrong Western software, into which was embedded a virus that corrupted and paralyzed their society for half a century.

One wonders why communism became so prevalent in East Asia in the latter part of the last century, while it never really caught on in Western Europe. I suspect the chief reason is that key elements of Asian culture made it easier for despots to deploy Marxist ideology in their own thirst for power. Confucianism stresses blind loyalty to authority, Taoism preaches moderation in the face of adversity, and Buddhism teaches suppression of selfishness. These three factors made East Asians more vulnerable to communist propaganda and mind-control. In contrast, Westerners, steeped in the soaring ideals of the Enlightenment, were much harder for dictators to subdue. It is essential to note that it was *communist dictators,* rather than communism per se, which were successful in Asia. Orientals and Occidentals may live in very different cultures, but prick them and they all bleed red. The human mind may be a product of both culture and biology, but when it comes to pain and suffering, biology trumps culture. Asians no more enjoy being subjugated, brutalized, and starved than anyone else. Pure communism, like pure Christianity, cannot work in Asia or anywhere else because it is not in human nature to love your fellow man as you would love yourself. People don't normally give away the sweat of their brow or turn the other cheek. Our minds have evolved to pass on our genes. Those whose genes are most like our own (ourselves, our children, and our siblings) are necessarily more important to us than are strangers. To love everyone equally, as Christ or Marx would have us do, is not in human nature. The ancient Chinese knew this better than anyone, hence the importance of family in the Confucian tradition. This was deliberately subverted by communist megalomaniacs like Mao, Pol Pot, and Kim Il Sung. They were more Machiavellian in the end, than Marxist.

Stalin, Mao, Kim Il Sung, and the Cambodian despot Pol Pot together killed over sixty million of their own people. It is ironic that four of the five worst mass murderers of modern times were leaders of "people's republics" that paid cynical lip service to the brotherhood of mankind.

North Korea is today the most authoritarian nation on earth. Twenty years after the disintegration of the Soviet Union, the isolated communist dictatorship remains a toxic legacy of ethnic nationalism infused with Marxist ideology. While China, Vietnam, and Cambodia have embraced free markets and liberalized their hold on society, albeit within a single party "communist" system, the so-called Democratic Peoples Republic of Korea remains a case apart. How did this failed state come about? Start with dynastic feudalism, Stalinist totalitarianism, ethnic nationalism, and xenophobic isolationism all within a geopolitical hot zone. Then add into this mix 24 million impoverished people with no experience of democracy, led by a paranoid megalomaniac with ready access to nuclear warheads, intercontinental ballistic missiles, and a military industrial complex that starves its citizens to feed its million-man army. What is like to live in North Korea? With its hermetically sealed society and Orwellian department of misinformation, it's difficult to separate fact from speculation. A good starting point is Barbara Demick's *Nothing to Envy: Ordinary Lives in North Korea*, an excellent collection of interviews with defectors. A brilliant fictionalized account, which isn't very far off the mark, is Adam Johnson's masterpiece of magical realism, *Orphan Master's Son*.

Nothing good ever comes out of this black hole of suffering: cyber-attacks on Sony, an American college student tortured into a coma, desperate laborers shipped out for slave labor, ICBM's allegedly capable of delivering a nuclear payload on Alaska. The United States has promised retaliation. The North Koreans have threatened to turn Seoul into a "sea of fire". The potential for escalation is real, but the nonchalant citizens of Seoul, used to such bombast signifying nothing in the end, are woefully unprepared for a full-scale artillery barrage, which is what would happen if the Americans launch a first strike on North Korean military assets.

There are no good options when it comes to dealing with North Korea. The trick is to find the least worst option, a fact further complicated by the differential utilitarian calculus of the players involved. First, for Kim Jung-un and his cronies, the goal is simply regime survival. They know that their impoverished terrorist state has no claim to legitimacy over the Korean people. They also know that their million-man army is so badly equipped that the Americans and South Koreans would quickly overwhelm them in a conventional war. The best they can hope for is a nuclear deterrent based on the Cold War doctrine of Mutual Assured Destruction. This requires the further development of a formidable arsenal of nuclear warheads mounted on multiple reliable delivery systems. Only then will their superior enemies leave them alone. After all, it worked for the Soviet Union for nearly half a century. Their mantra may well be "peace through strength".

The Americans cannot tolerate this sort of escalation precisely because the threat to a major urban population center is coming from an inherently inferior adversary. North Korea is not a first among equals. Allowing Kim Jung-un to establish a nuclear deterrent is to encourage any other rogue state or terrorist network to similarly arm itself and extort the United States and its allies. The solution is to threaten, cajole, and if all else fails, provoke a conflict before such an asymmetric deterrent can be implemented. A winnable conflict is preferable to a peace dictated by a nuclear-armed North Korea that may destroy you later. If the Trump administration believes such a conflict is still winnable, they will feel pressured to provoke one. Better to sacrifice Seoul now than Los Angeles later. Their mantra is "better to cut your losses".

Most South Koreans have good reason to disagree. Seoul is less than forty miles from the DMZ, and within striking range of North Korean artillery. According to some estimates, in the event of a full scale North Korean attack, perhaps twenty thousand South Korean civilians would be killed within the first few hours. The casualties will then decrease as the survivors finally find their way into the city's vast network of bomb shelters. A nuclear attack would alter this picture dramatically, with perhaps a hundred thousand or more dead. This is not a price worth paying even if the Americans win the Second Korean War and unify the peninsula. The South Korean maxim may well be: "no war brings peace".

President Trump may be willing to take the wager of a limited military strike over the risk of a future North Korean nuclear attack on American soil. This makes sense in terms of protecting American lives. Most of us, and not just Koreans (on both sides), would disagree. Yet the alternative is to wait for a collapse from within. Given the historic resilience of the

Pyongyang regime and the Korean people's limitless capacity to tolerate suffering, this is unlikely happen before hundreds of thousands, perhaps millions, die untimely deaths. From a utilitarian standpoint, doing nothing may be the worst option of all. Once again, we see that Asians are their own worst enemy.

Breaking the Bamboo Ceiling

All good things must come to an end. Eventually the West became a victim of its own success. Two of its most brilliant achievements, science and consumer capitalism, contained the seeds of decline. Starting in the late nineteenth century, the skepticism bred of scientific inquiry, what Charles Murray calls "post-Darwin secularism", undermined religious faith. Most people already lived rather secular lives anyway, and the work ethic had shifted away from its religious rubric, so the economic indices of the European powers continued to shoot up with the industrial revolution. But the Christian grounding that gave most Europeans a sense of purpose was fast disappearing. When Friedrich Nietzsche declared God dead in *Also Sprach Zarathustra*, there was not much left to fill the spiritual vacuum.

In the twentieth century, this vacuum was filled with consumer capitalism and its endless pursuit of pleasure. Victorian entrepreneurs dreamed of getting rich by convincing the masses to covet the products and lifestyles of modernity. A century later, this had become reality. God was supplanted by the shopping mall and the ATM. Materialism became the new spiritualism.

Great achievement requires more than just motivation; it takes a sense of autonomy and purpose. It need not come from religion, but it should come from something more inspired than Wal-Mart. To quote Charles Murray, "after Freud, Nietzsche, and others with similar messages, the belief in man as rational and volitional took a body blow. It became fashionable in the Europe of the early twentieth century to see humans as unwittingly acting out neuroses and subconscious drives. God was mostly dead among the European creative elites; morality became relative. These and allied beliefs substantially undermined the belief of creative elites that their lives had purpose or that their talents could be efficacious." Science and capitalism conspired to bring down the Protestant work ethic. Without faith in itself, Western culture boiled down to an unbearable lightness of mindless consumerism and irresponsible hedonism.

The most remarkable socio-cultural transformation in recent history has been the modernization (and Westernization) of East Asia. Take a trip to any of the dazzling mega-cities of the Pacific Rim, Shanghai, Saigon, Singapore, Seoul, Jakarta, Hong Kong, Taipei and see for yourself. Skyscrapers, smart phones, and Starbucks have replaced rickshaws and tin shacks. At night, the streets are bathed in LED rainbows. Armies of workers still stream to work each morning with the discipline of their grandfathers, but now they rush into subways dressed in sharp suits armed with the latest Samsung tablet. The air is electric with the buzz of the global network. Asia now seems more alive than anywhere else on the planet.

If you could take a trip back to these places in the summer of 1945, the difference would be striking. All of them were still part of the Japanese "co-prosperity sphere". But there was no prosperity to speak of. Civil unrest and the specter of communism loomed so large that the victorious Americans and British considered allowing defeated Japanese troops to maintain security. Eventually, in line with America's wartime anti-imperial stance, Asia was given back to the Asians.

What East and Southeast Asians did with their newfound freedom can be divided into two categories: extreme Communism and extreme Capitalism, derived from the competing European teams of Karl Marx and Adam Smith. North Korea and Singapore exemplify this dichotomy best. The Asians blended both of those alien ideologies with indigenous Confucian and Buddhist values of filial obligation, respect for tradition, and selfless perseverance, to create novel kinds of social, political, and economic systems. Within a half-century, the world's most oppressive Stalinist dictatorship, the largest communist state, and the second and third biggest capitalist economies were all sharing the same stretch of the East China Sea.

The economic transformation of China over the last four decades may someday be regarded as the most significant cultural phenomenon of its age, perhaps even on par with the rise of Europe five centuries before. The Chinese never embraced individualism, but they had faith in their

Confucian values. There were occasions in their long history when that faith was shaken, most recently under the specter of Marxism. It was a dark time without the respect for autonomy, and without the solace of faith: the worst of both worlds. But now at a moment when the West is losing faith in itself, the East seems to be regaining it. There is a double irony here when we recall the events of the fifteenth century when the Ming Emperor retreated from the world at the very moment when Europeans started to venture forth into it. The Asian reawakening is a process that started with the Japanese a century ago, continued a half-century later with the little tigers of Hong Kong, Singapore, Taiwan, and Korea, and has now spread to the Chinese motherland. Can the Chinese download the fruits of Western success without embracing the individualism that went into making it possible? And if they do embrace it, will they eventually lose faith in what made them strong? Autonomy is powerfully addictive. Once hooked, the user is capable of great things, but eventually it can ruin his health. Can it be taken in moderation?

If the bamboo ceiling is to be broken, Asians and their diaspora cannot rely on their Confucian values alone. Cramming Western knowledge or aping Western style is not enough. They must embrace the liberating power of Western traditions: individualism, competition, science, free enterprise, and democracy, and ground them in Asian values: cooperation, discipline, hard work, and respect for teachers. Steven Chu, physicist, molecular biologist, Nobel laureate and former Energy Secretary for the Obama Administration, exemplifies this well. The child of Chinese immigrants and scholars, Chu studied at Berkeley, where he developed maverick ideas about global warming and how to combat it before anyone else thought it was an issue. Chu never learned to speak Mandarin as a child, and is now married to an Oxford-educated British physicist. But he credits his achievements to his Confucian upbringing. The bamboo ceiling will be shattered by those like him who can most skillfully blend the best of the East with the best of the West.

5

Who's Your Daddy?
Orphans, Half-Breeds & Ethnic Nationalism

> It is better to be feared than loved, if you cannot be both.
> Niccolo Machiavelli

> Culture is not an excuse to abuse human rights.
> Jane Jeong Trenka
> Adoptee & advocate

When I was in the fifth grade in Mississippi, there was a boy in my class who had been adopted from a Korean orphanage by a white family. We became friends and I sometimes biked to his house to play with him and his two white sisters. One day, I exclaimed to his mother, "Isn't it great that we both come from the same country?" I remember her glaring at me with an unmistakable look of displeasure. I never mentioned it again.

Two years later, in New Jersey, there was a girl in my class whose mother was Korean and her father a white American soldier who had been stationed at an army base in Seoul in the 60's. When I asked my mother if it was okay to do homework together with the girl, she told me I shouldn't hang out with low class mixed-race kids.

These two examples from my childhood encapsulate the complex, often emotionally fraught relationship among adopted Koreans, their Caucasian parents, multiracial Korean-Americans, and first and second-generation Korean immigrants. Being adopted often brings up issues of loss and belonging, but being adopted into a different racial background makes it even more difficult. In this chapter I will first discuss the unique experience of growing up as an adopted or biracial Korean in white America and how it profoundly challenges one's sense of self-identity. Then I will discuss the root cause of social displacement in Korean culture: *ethnic nationalism.*

Orphans

Most Americans who grew up in the 70's or later can probably recall the lone Asian kid in homeroom with the white-sounding name and Midwestern accent, who was shunned in gym class and teased by bullies who taunted him with names like "Ching Chong". Chances are he was probably adopted from Korea. Between the end of the Korean War in 1953 and 2008, over 160,000 abandoned children were adopted abroad. 110,000 of them went to the United States, making them the largest contingent of foreign adoptees in American history. Around 10,000 orphans each also ended up in France, Denmark, and Sweden, and sizable contingents were sent to Norway, Holland, Germany, Belgium, Australia, and Switzerland. The numbers were small at first, but gradually swelled to a peak in 1995, when over 8800 Korean children were adopted overseas. The numbers have gone down since, but still over a thousand were adopted in 2010. It is estimated that a tenth of the Korean population of the United States is now composed of Korean adoptees and their children.

It's easy to understand why children are adopted from war-torn nations. The Korean holocaust left hundreds of thousands of orphans as collateral damage. Compassionate GI's and their families started to take some of these waifs home, legally or otherwise. By 1956, Harry Holt's adoption agency was doing brisk business providing American couples with cute little Koreans for a reasonable fee. At first, most of those kids really were orphans whose parents had perished in the war. But this was no longer the case by the late 90's, when the orphan export was at its peak. Korea had by then become a vibrant, prosperous country whose wartime memories had faded, and whose mantra was "an Internet connection in every home". It's an irony that a nation blessed with double-digit economic growth and plagued by a declining birth rate still felt it necessary to outsource thousands of its children to foreigners. We will return to this paradox of Korean culture later.

What is it like for an Asian child to grow up with Caucasian parents? A recent survey of adult Korean-American adoptees sponsored by the Evan Donaldson Adoption Institute found that 78% of respondents considered themselves white or had wanted to be white as children. By the time they reached their thirties, however, over 60% of them had traveled to Korea to explore the culture of their homeland or to find their birth parents. These are telling statistics.

In the early days of transnational adoptions, parents were encouraged to sever their children from all reminders of their terrible lives in the old country. No Korean was spoken, no kimchi was served, Cha Jung Hee was christened Deann Borshay, and Yoo Chang Ho morphed into Jonathan Carfield. Things seemed okay at first because baby brains are plastic. If cultural transformation is what you want, nothing beats the total immersion method. Within a few years, over a hundred thousand abandoned Korean waifs became as American as apple pie. But the problem is that speaking, acting, thinking, and dressing like white kids in Minnesota doesn't also make you look like one. A recurrent theme voiced by many Korean adoptees was the strangely disconcerting feeling they got when they saw themselves in the mirror. One adoptee said that she felt like a white person trapped in an Asian body. Some adoptees responded by denial: dating only white people, avoiding Asian restaurants, making fun of Koreans "fresh off the boat". But denial can only work for so long. Most adoptees eventually felt the need to come to grips with their racial identity.

In her heartbreaking documentary, *First Person Plural*, filmmaker Deann Borshay travels to Korea in search of her biological family. She eventually reunites with her mother, but to their mutual frustration, the two cannot understand each other. Even beyond the formidable language barrier, there is a yawning cultural chasm that separates them. In a particularly poignant scene, Borshay's Korean mother tells her daughter that she only gave birth to her, but that her adoptive parents are "more real" because they made her into who she is, and that she should go back to them. The feeling of rejection is overwhelming for Ms. Borshay and she breaks down sobbing. Earlier, she observed that going back to Korea and seeing people who looked like her made her feel oddly at home, while her adoptive parents, upon whom she had once depended on for survival, seemed like elderly white strangers.

The psychology of identity comes from a congruence of genotype (racial features) and phenotype (cultural endowment). Korean adoptees raised in an American or European culture experience a mismatch between physical appearance and cultural affinity. This is also largely true for the children and grandchildren of Asian immigrants. But most latter generation Asian Americans still have some cultural sense of being Asian; even if they are unable to speak Korean and have never visited Asia, their parents and grandparents can endow them with "virtual memories". Adoptees lack even this tenuous link. Enlightened liberal adoptive parents may send their kids to Korean cultural camps or Tae Kwon Do class, but it doesn't really give them a Korean identity. The descendants of Korean immigrants are cultural hybrids. Despite prejudice and adjustment difficulties, they know who they are because they know where they're from. Korean adoptees may be biologically Asian, but they have no cultural link.

Each year, thousands of overseas Korean adoptees make the pilgrimage to South Korea. Some impulsively drop out of school, quit high paying jobs, or leave their supportive families behind with little planning and no sense of direction. Jonathan Yoo Carfield, as profiled in the *I Am Korean American* website, is a case in point. Adopted at the age of three, he grew up on a farm in rural Nebraska, and eventually became a financial analyst for a venture capital firm in Manhattan. "However, I later realized that fancy suits and expensive dinner reservations wasn't really me...so I left New York to move to the country that I was from, but knew very little about, South Korea." He adds, "I've been in Seoul for the last 20 months and I'm still not sure what I'm doing here." Many returning adoptees struggle to fit into a culture that is at once both inscrutable and unwelcoming to outsiders. Even those lucky few who manage to reunite with their biological families are not immune to alienation.

Every case is different. Toby Dawson, a professional freestyle skier who won a Bronze Medal at the 2006 Winter Olympic Games in Torino, was born Kim Bong-seok in Pusan in 1978. At the age of three, he was separated from his mother at a busy market, picked up by a local orphanage, and eventually adopted by a family of ski instructors in Colorado. After his exploits at the Olympics were broadcast on Korean television, several men came forward claiming that Toby was their son. Fortunately, Toby did find his real parents and younger brother and is now the assistant coach of the South Korean ski team. Happy endings like his are relatively rare. Most adoptees never find their parents. And many of those who do, like Deann Borshay, remain frustrated by linguistic and cultural gaps. But perhaps an even larger hurdle to true reconciliation may be an atmosphere of intolerance inherent in Korean society.

In her book, *Adopted Territory: Transnational Korean Adoptees and the Politics of Belonging*, anthropologist Eleana Kim describes an incident that happened to Craig Adams, a young Korean adoptee from Wisconsin who spent the summer of 2004 in Seoul teaching English and learning about Korean culture. While talking to some white American friends on a subway, Adams was approached by a middle-aged Korean man who became very irate when Adams ignored him. "I just wanted to be able to tell him, 'I'm sorry, I was adopted. I can't speak Korean.'" Ethnic Koreans, whether adopted or the offspring of immigrants, are often made to feel uncomfortable upon visiting their homeland because they are not considered sufficiently Korean. Because they look Korean, they are expected to act like one too. Korean cultural exclusion extends to many other out-groups as well. Particularly vicious is the prejudice directed against mixed-race Koreans.

Half-Breeds

In the sixty plus years since the armistice that paused the Korean War, thousands of South Korean women have been impregnated by American soldiers who were deployed there to defend them against North Korean aggression. Many of these women gave birth to black children. One of them was Hines Ward, who became a popular wide receiver for the Pittsburgh Steelers and, in 2006, went on to win the MVP award in Super Bowl XL. Ward's mother, Kim Yong He, was disowned by her family and ostracized by her Korean neighbors for having a child with a black man. But the trouble didn't stop after the family moved to Georgia. Ward's parents soon divorced and the boy was raised in poverty by his mother, who spoke little

English. "It was hard for me to find my identity. The black kids didn't want to hang out with me because I had a Korean mom. The white kids didn't want to hang out with me because I was black. The Korean kids didn't want to hang out with me because I was black. It was hard to find friends growing up." Growing up interracial in rural America wasn't easy. But it's nothing compared to what mixed race children in Korea have to go through even today. As sportswriter John Branch writes in a New York Times article about Hines Ward (The Journey Towards Acceptance, NYT, Nov 9, 2009):

> "There was a boy who was bullied into depression and tried to commit suicide. There was a girl ordered by a teacher to keep her hair pulled back tight, to straighten the natural curls she inherited from her black father. There was another too intimidated by her taunting classmates to board the bus, choosing instead the humiliating and lonely walk to school. There were the boys who were beaten regularly and teased mercilessly. There were college-age girls who broke into tears when telling their stories of growing up biracial in South Korea."

Fortunately, these Amerasian kids profiled by Branch were flown to Pittsburgh and given an audience with Ward through the Pearl S. Buck International, a philanthropic society dedicated to the welfare of biracial children in Korea. Their peers back home now envy them. People like Hines Ward, Toby Dawson, and Ben Henderson, a champion mixed martial artist whose father was an African-American GI, have become national heroes in Korea, perhaps more popular there than in America. But "half-breed" children who are not so famous continue to be bullied to the point of suicide. The hypocrisy is remarkable.

Biracial Koreans in the United States may not face that kind of prejudice, but neither are they immune to issues of identity. In Southern California, a group of them started to meet annually since 2009 through the website *halfKorean.com*. This is what one of them had to say:

"When I was 14 years old, I had a really bad experience. I really liked an Asian girl, but a lot of people gossiped that I was half-white, and that white people are stupid...I was really hurt. Being half-Korean, it's hard, you're very isolated. One day on Google, I typed in "half-Korean" and I was amazed, all the half-Korean people, it was beautiful. [It was] one of the happiest days of my life. This needed to happen a long time ago. If this had existed in the fifties, the 50,000 half-Korean kids that were found in public toilets, left on doorsteps, found dumped on the docks, in the ocean, might not have happened, right?"

Similar groups of Korean adoptees gather regularly throughout the United States and Europe, and thousands of them congregate annually in Seoul, much to the curiosity of the South Koreans. The stated goal at each of these meetings is to socialize and network, but these gatherings serve a larger purpose: they instill a sense of identity through shared community. No matter how loved and accepted they may have been in the West, many adoptees and half-breeds don't feel totally at home there. But in Korea, they are made to feel like foreigners. Racially disconnected in one setting and culturally disconnected in the other, they are twice alienated. Gathering with others like themselves allows them to forge their own special identity.

In-Groups and Out-Groups

Koreans are among the most intolerant people in the world. In a much publicized case from the summer of 2009, a visiting Indian engineering professor named Bonojit Hussain and his female Korean companion were harassed on a Seoul bus by a man who shouted, "how does it feel to be dating a stinking black bastard?" When Hussain reported the incident to the local police, the officers took the Korean man's side. There are many stories of Koreans picking fights in bars and restaurants with white men accompanied by Korean girlfriends. Homosexuals, foreign guest workers, Vietnamese mail order brides, North Korean refugees, biracial children, orphans, single mothers, and communists have all been victims of systematic prejudice. In international rankings of women's rights, South

Korea has consistently ranked near the bottom of the list. And, of course, the relationship between the two Korean states remains utterly dysfunctional. Why are Koreans so heartless? To answer this loaded question we need to understand the neuroscience of *in-group/out-group biases.*

In the second chapter, I described the distinction between *empathizing* (affective empathy) and *mentalizing* (cognitive empathy). The first is the natural ability to channel another person's emotional state, allowing one to vicariously feel another's pain, for instance. Affective empathy is automatic, largely subconscious, and mediated by resonating *mirror neuron* activity in two midline regions of the brain, the *anterior insula* (AI) and the *anterior cingulate cortex* (ACC). Cognitive empathy, on the other hand, is an acquired trait that involves understanding someone else's *theory of mind.* It is associated with activity in the *medial prefrontal cortex* (mPFC) and the *temporoparietal junction* (TPJ) bilaterally. These separate mental modules allow individuals to connect with their social network in two distinct ways.

People are more likely to feel compassion for those closer to them (family members, friends, neighbors, countrymen) than for strangers or foreigners. We tend to like those who are more like us. Neuroscientists have now found signatures of brain activity corresponding to differential empathy. In one study, African American test subjects were shown pictures of strangers, some black and some white, suffering in the aftermath of Hurricane Katrina. Irrespective of the victim's race, the test subjects' brain images revealed equally increased activity in the AI and ACC. The ability to feel bad for others is hardwired into the human brain. But what's interesting is that activity in the TPJ and mPFC, the theory of mind centers, was greater when the subjects were shown pictures of victims of *their own race.* In other words, while affective empathy is evoked equally in response to universal suffering, cognitive empathy is preferentially deployed in response to the suffering of in-group members.

East Asian cultures are more rigidly hierarchical than modern Western societies that embrace autonomy and egalitarianism. Is it possible that life in a hierarchical society blunts the expression of empathy? The answer is complex. Asians do score higher on measures of social dominance orientation, but also demonstrate more in-group empathy bias than Caucasians. This makes sense. In-group biases protect the integrity of authority, while loyalty to authority figures produces the in-group bias. The cohesion of the group requires the rule of authority. This is something conservatives know very well. There can be no "in-groups", by definition, in a culture that is truly egalitarian. If you felt equally close to everyone, than those closest to you would not be close at all. This goes against the human grain, and is a major reason why communism fails.

Cultural neuroscientist Joan Chiao of Northwestern University has looked at differences between Koreans and Westerners using cross-cultural neuroimaging. The results are intriguing. We know that Koreans are less egalitarian and more hierarchical. What's interesting is that they tend to demonstrate *decreased* activity in the AI and ACC on fMRI scans overall in response to emotional stimuli than Caucasians. In other words, they are emotionally reticent group players. The stereotype of the expressionless and inscrutable Asian face may have some truth to it. But in-group biases show a *positive correlation* with both social dominance orientation and activity in the TPJ, all of which are greater for Koreans than for Westerners. This implies that while Koreans feel less affective empathy for outsiders, they may be better at understanding what others are thinking. Westerners, in contrast, are better at feeling others' emotions regardless of group affiliation. Ecological and historical factors have given Koreans (and East Asians in general) a strong sense of self-identity and social hierarchy that makes them dependable group players. But the flip side of in-group solidarity is a xenophobic animosity towards outgroups, a problem that has threatened the very existence of the Korean people over the last century.

Daehan Minguk = Danil Minjok

In the autumn of 1990, I made my first trip to Berlin with a rucksack on my back and eurorail pass in hand. Germany had just been reunified. Near the Brandenberg Gate, I casually took a photo of the Reichstag through a hole that been punched through the Wall. On one side was a poster for the united colors of Benetton: "come together" under a picture of a smiling biracial couple. On the other side someone had scrawled something in Korean that I made out only years later: "*daum un daehan minguk*" (next is Korea). The once mighty Soviet Union, which created its North Korean puppet state in 1947, has fallen into the dustbin of history.

Over a quarter century later, the Korean peninsula remains more bitterly divided then ever.

Throughout their long history, the Korean people have acquired a reputation for suffering, usually at the hands of their larger neighbors, the Chinese and Japanese. But they are also considered obstinate, hot-tempered, hard-drinking and self-hating, earning them the dubious moniker, "the Irish of Asia". When I was a little boy, my mother used to tell me a fable about a frog who compulsively disobeyed his mother. Whatever she implored him to do, he would do the exact opposite. One day she falls gravely ill. She wants more than anything to be buried on the mountaintop with her ancestors. But on her deathbed she comes to realize that her willful son will probably do just the opposite, so she tells him instead to lay her body to rest in the swift flowing river. Suddenly filled with tears of remorse, the son actually obeys his mother's final wish. This is why, to this day, you can hear the mountain frog crying by the riverbank.

Two thousand three hundred thirty three years before Jesus Christ walked in Galilee, the god-hero Dangun made his descent onto the Heavenly Lake atop Mount Baekdu (now on the Chinese-North Korean border), merged with the people of Manchuria, and gave birth to the Korean race. So goes historiographer and nationalist Shin Chae-Ho's reinterpretation of the origin myth chronicled in the medieval *Samguk Yusa*. Shin (1880-1936) wrote his influential *Joeseon Sanggosa* (Early History of Korea) in 1925 while the entire peninsula was under Japanese oppression. The revised Dangun myth implies that all Koreans are related not just through common language and culture, but also through a shared bloodline dating back to the *Goguryeo Dynasty* centered in Manchuria. According to this line of reasoning, modern Koreans are the survivors of thousands of years of competition amongst the three ancient Kingdoms (Goguryeo, Silla, and Paekche) and their foreign neighbors.

Shin captured the imagination of a generation of Korean freedom fighters by framing the Korean foundation myth in racial terms and combining it with the new philosophy of Social Darwinism. Among them was Yi Kwang-Su (1892-1950), novelist, intellectual, and author of "Theory of the Korean Nation" (1933). In it, he conceived of the Korean state in Hegelian terms as an organic being defined by common bloodline, personality, and culture. Yi took Shin's concept of Korean racial identity and merged it with the notion of modern nationalism. *Ethnic nationalism,* the political ideology that defines a nation in terms of both shared ethnicity (language and culture) and racial origin, was popular in the first half of the twentieth century. The militaristic ambitions of both Nazi Germany and Imperial Japan were based on it. In fact, it was Meiji era Japanese who introduced the concept of *danil minjok,* loosely translated as "race-nation", to Koreans around the turn of the century in an effort to recruit them as junior members of the master race destined to rule over East Asia. Both Shin and Yi were active in the Korean provisional government established in Shanghai after the massive 1919 independence rallies, in which as many as 7,000 demonstrators were reportedly killed by Japanese riot police. But while Shin remained committed to the resistance, and died in Japanese captivity in Taiwan, Yi, a more complex figure, later became a collaborator and was executed for treason by the North Korean army.

When the Americans Toby Dawson and Hines Ward triumphed on the ski slopes and the gridiron, Koreans cheered them as their own. When Cho Seung-Hui, a naturalized American citizen since childhood, gunned down 32 people at Virginia Tech in what was then the worst single shooter mass murder in American history, the South Korean government felt the need to issue a formal apology. When Jim Yong Kim, a Harvard trained physician and anthropologist who moved to Iowa with his parents at age five, was selected as president of the World Bank, people in Seoul were filled with pride. On the other hand, ethnic Filipinos who have lived and worked in Korea all their lives and speak flawless Korean are still treated like foreigners. All this would probably seem strange to most white Americans, who are more likely to identify themselves by nationality than ethnicity. They are Americans first, and Irish, Italian, Catholic, Jewish, Armenian, or Polish second. But Koreans, on both sides of the peninsula and overseas, are obsessed by "purity of blood". It is shameful for Koreans to be tainted by Chinese, Japanese, Caucasian, or, especially, black African blood. The North Koreans pride themselves on being "the cleanest race". For them, nationality is defined by *jus sanguinis,* the right of birth. Koreans may have acquired their exaggerated in-group/out-group differences for two reasons. First is genetic homogeneity, which tends to produce phenotypic similarity, psychological conservatism, and cultural xenophobia. This is true of many cultures, including those prevailing in rural parts of the United States (the so called "red states"), and, indeed, in most of the non-Western world. The second source of in-group/out-group emphasis was the unique historical trauma of Japanese colonialism.

King Sejong gave the Koreans a wonderful alphabet (*hangul*) in the mid fifteenth century. Old Korean (written in Chinese characters) was spoken starting in the twelfth century. And proto-Korean dates from the ancient Silla Kingdom, founded in the first century BC. The Korean people have had a distinctive identity for a very long time. But Dangun mythology aside, Korean culture and genes didn't rain down on Mount Baekdu like manna from the heavens. Linguists tell us that Korean belongs to the *Altaic* language family, which includes Mongolian, Japanese, and Turkish. Spoken Korean and Japanese are, in fact, quite closely related grammatically, despite phonetic differences. And geneticists tell us that Korean Y chromosome and mitochondrial sequences are commonly found in Manchurian populations, while their autosomal markers are largely indistinguishable from those found in Japanese populations. Far from being racially unique, Koreans share common ancestors with all the people of East Asia. It is not surprising then that they share hierarchical social structures and in-group prejudices with neighboring societies.

The Korean brand of ethnic nationalism turned out to be even more extreme than those of its neighbors thanks to Imperial Japan's existential threat to Korean cultural identity during its occupation from 1910 to 1945. It was at this time that danil minjok developed into a kind of survival tactic. An entire people may have their citizenship revoked, their government dissolved, the teaching of their language banned, and even their names forcibly changed, but for those who believe in their *essence,* self-identity cannot be expunged. This explains why the myth of Korean racial exceptionalism typified by works like Joeseon Sanggosa became so readily accepted in the early decades of the twentieth century. The combination of traditional in-group preference with the new blood and soil mythology produced a quasi-fascist ideology. But unlike Japanese fascism and German Nazism, which were both obliterated in the Second World War, Korean ethnic nationalism only grew stronger as the Japanese tightened their wartime stranglehold on the peninsula.

During the war, thousands of nationalists were executed, tens of thousands of girls and young women forced into sexual servitude, and hundreds of thousands of young men pressed into the Japanese military. Among them was Yang Kyoung-jong, whose remarkable story forms the prelude to British military historian Antony Beevor's *Second World War*. In 1938, eighteen year-old Yang was drafted into the Kwantung Army defending the Manchurian frontier against the Soviet Red Army. After their victory in the Battle of Khalkhin Gol the following year, the Russians took him prisoner. He spent three years in a Siberian prison camp before being recruited into the struggling Red Army just in time to be captured by the advancing Wehrmacht in the Battle of Kharkov. Soon facing a manpower shortage of their own, the Germans then conscripted him to defend the Normandy beaches against the impending allied invasion. Yang was captured a third time by troops of the American 101st Airborne Division, who mistook him for a Japanese soldier in German uniform. After a stint in a British POW camp, this man without a country was finally allowed to settle down in the United States. He died peacefully in Illinois in 1992. His story is unusual, but it reflects the desperate rootlessness of a people shorn of their nationality.

Danil minjok may have served a purpose during the Japanese occupation, but it proved self-destructive afterwards. Like the allegory of the frog, it was a good intention deployed too late. Ethnic nationalism needs an out-group. With their colonial oppressors out of the picture following the annihilation of Hiroshima, the Korean people soon turned on each other in an orgy of violence and vengeance that left over three million of them dead, millions more homeless, and their homeland shattered and divided as it had never been under the Japanese occupation. I find it ironic that a people that considers itself to be of one blood suffers the most irreconcilable national division in the world today. But then some of the bitterest animosities have historically been between groups who are really quite similar such as Serbs and Croats of the former Yugoslavia, Sunni and Shiite Muslims of Iraq, and Protestants and Catholics of Northern Ireland. Like many other oppressed peoples, the Koreans take excessive pride in their culture. It's a survival trait that enabled them to cling so tenaciously to their identity through two thousand years of adversity. The flip side of that strong identity is the xenophobia and intolerance for outsiders that earned them the sobriquet, the "hermit kingdom". But the tragedy of the last seventy years of Korean history is that most of those victimized "outsiders" have been other Koreans.

Foreign Koreans

I was born in Seoul, but raised by North Koreans. My mother came from a well-to-do family in the town of Kaechon, about fifty miles north of Pyongyang. They were friendly enough with the Japanese to operate a lucrative factory in the Chinese city of Harbin, also under Japanese control. All that was lost when the Soviets invaded Manchuria in the summer of 1945. In fact, Russian troops had made it all the way down to the 38th parallel and were beginning to seal off the their zone of occupation. They recruited a charismatic 33 year-old resistance fighter named Kim Il-sung to lead the communist revolution. Roving bands of armed youths went house-to-house harassing landowners, government officials, and the educated elite. My grandparents knew it was time to leave when they got an unwelcome knock on their door from a club-wielding thug. A few days later, my mother's grandfather bribed a local fisherman with most of his life savings. Sneaking out after midnight with little more than the clothes on their backs, the entire extended family, including my grandmother nursing her eight-month-old daughter, set off on their harrowing ordeal. As the story goes, the overcrowded boat nearly capsized in a typhoon. After four days on the high seas, they made it to the port of Inchon, terrified and exhausted, but alive. It was time to start over.

Theirs was a fate shared by millions of northerners who happened to get caught on the wrong side of an imaginary line drawn up by a couple of junior officers in the State Department. The people of Kaechon were no more likely to be pro-Soviet communists than the people of Inchon were to be pro-American capitalists. But once the arbitrary division took hold, local leaders on both sides immediately took advantage of their people's natural proclivity for Confucian hierarchy, unquestioning obedience to authority, in-group solidarity and out-group hostility by ratcheting up the propaganda machine and channeling their inner minjok. The mutual demonization had begun. It is remarkable how quickly and thoroughly the brainwashing worked on both sides. In the early days of the Korean War, an untold number of civilians was massacred by enthusiastic local militias given orders to root out either communists or right-wing nationalists. There were atrocities on all sides including the notorious incident at the village of No Gun Ri in the summer of 1950, where American fighter planes strafed fleeing Korean refugees, killing as many as 300 women and children. But that pales in comparison to the actions of the South Korean army, which summarily executed tens of thousands of suspected communists and other left-leaning sympathizers the same year.

The wholesale denial of human rights in the nightmarishly oppressive Democratic People's Republic of Korea stands in stark contrast to the vibrant democracy in its sister state. But it is easy to forget that democracy is a new concept to South Koreans. Theirs was a nation ruled by a succession of military dictators until 1992, most notably President Park Chung-hee. During much of this time, political opponents and communist sympathizers were often jailed and/or tortured without due process on the dubious grounds of national security. In both Koreas, the welfare of the state has historically eclipsed the rights of its individuals.

Inside Out-groups

The callous disregard for the welfare of fellow citizens is indicative of a deeper aspect of the Korean psyche. My mother, who as an infant refugee made it to the south in a leaky boat and has lived in America since 1973, once told me that Koreans are "don't care about strangers." This crude generalization was widely cited by African Americans as a reason for burning down Koreatown during the Los Angeles riots in 1992. Korean society is so obsessed by respect that its language uses a different set of words to address people of higher status, yet it demonstrates little sympathy for its less fortunate members. Koreans respect social status not out of compassion for strangers, but to satisfy obligation to the group.

To be fair, South Korea has come a long way. A backward feudal kingdom just a century ago is now an evolving democracy and home of the world's ninth largest economy. But Confucian values have fallen by the wayside in the mad dash for progress. Duty and sacrifice have given way to crass consumerism. This has serious implications for the prospect of national reunification. Recent polls indicate that less than thirty percent of South Koreans want unification with their northern neighbor. In 1990, that figure was near ninety percent. The problem has less to do with the fear of war or communism than with the cost of supporting their destitute cousins. As the columnist Sonu Jong wrote in Korea's largest newspaper, *Chosun Ilbo:*

> "I am quite nervous at the thought of some strangers from North Korea knocking at my door after reunification telling me they are my relatives. I am concerned about the streets of Seoul being filled with poor and disillusioned strangers from the north. I believe that reunification should have occurred during my father's generation, when there were people who really wanted it to happen. We may have been poorer, but there were many more people back then who were willing to share what little they had. If we are more concerned about the share price of Samsung Electronics then we are about reunification, then we will never be able to become one nation."

Selfish attitudes may be expected from the *nouveau riche*. But what makes the Korean situation particularly bad is the addition of a uniquely narrow-minded prejudice directed at an "inside" out-group. It is so difficult to get out of North Korea that in the forty years following the end of the Korean War, less than three thousand successfully escaped to the south. In the decades of desperation following the collapse of the Soviet Union in 1993, that number swelled to 25,000.

Upon arrival, defectors are debriefed and "re-educated" for a life in the free world. The South Korean government prides itself on giving them a small living allowance and affirmative action benefits for work and study. But some never find their way. Many end up unemployed and homeless, unable to adjust to the pace and complexity of a modern capitalist society. But a significant part of the problem lies in the callous way South Koreans treat their refugees. Unlike returning adoptees, North Koreans speak the same language. But they too are never really made to feel at home. They're considered lazy for failing to assert themselves after lifetimes of coerced obedience. They're called stupid for failing to grasp the cultural references they missed while attending communist rallies. They're teased for being short in stature as a result of growing up on starvation rations. They're dismissed as tax drains, when southerners spend much more on pursuits like plastic surgery and K-Pop. Many refugees, after surviving deprivation, separation from family, and the constant threat of torture and worse, make it to South Korea only to become depressed in the midst of material bounty. If this country cannot handle 25,000 refugees, how can it possibly handle the 25 million North Koreans it seeks to liberate?

The targets of Korean narrow-mindedness are not limited to communists and refugees; it's an attitude that crosses the boundaries of age, race, class, and sex. Let's examine each of them. For Koreans, like other Asians, the family is the ultimate in-group. Parents think nothing of sacrificing their hard-earned savings on cram schools for their children, sometimes sending them overseas for years at a time so that they can learn English and improve their chances of getting into a good university and landing a high paying job. This devotional mindset stems partly from the Taoist/Buddhist ideal that views children as extensions of their parents. It's much easier (and less selfless) to be good your children when they are literally a part of you. But a more practical reason lies in the Confucian belief that children are the best insurance policy for old age. Do as much as you can for your children, because it will (hopefully) all come back to you, with interest, in the end. It was the social contract between the generations, and not ethnic nationalism, that held Korean society together for thousands of years. In a nation with few nursing homes and hardly any social security, the elderly were well cared for by the children to whom so much was given and so much was expected.

The arrival of Western consumer culture upset this balance. Today, children grow up in a hypercompetitive environment in which the pressure to succeed often ends in burnout. Young adults in Korea work longer hours than most of their counterparts in the West, and are often too busy to spend much time with their aging parents. The days of extended families sitting on the *ondol*-heated floor enjoying grandfather's dinnertime tales are long gone. South Korea is now suffering an epidemic of geriatric suicide as well, whose rate is among the highest in the world. The elderly feel increasingly abandoned by their children and cheated out of a system that worked so well for their own parents.

Biracial Koreans suffer from the same racism that marginalizes foreign migrant workers. Koreans are less likely to discriminate against Caucasians, particularly English speakers, whom many subconsciously view as superior to themselves. Southeast Asians are given no such regard, and the dark complexioned people of Africa and South Asia suffer most of all. Given this racial gradient, it's not surprising that biracial children of black fathers and Korean mothers are particularly shunned. The fortunate ones, like Hines Ward, immigrate to America. Many of those who remain eventually gravitate to Seoul's Itaewon district, where they find security in numbers. Some, like the R&B singer Insooni, have managed to become famous.

Itaewon is an interesting place. Bordering an American military base and the embassy district, it had a cosmopolitan feel long before the rest of Seoul went *Gangnam Style*. Foreign troops used to hang out on its seedy streets to buy drugs and pick up prostitutes. Today, it's a combination of frenzied shopping mall and countercultural enclave, where mixed-race impresarios and lesbian bartenders rub shoulders with expats and tourists. Americans seem to love it as much as conservative Koreans despise it. Seedy decadence aside, Itaewon's unmistakable atmosphere of tolerance, reminiscent of Berkeley's Telegraph Avenue and New York's East Village, is naturally attractive for multiethnics, homosexuals, returning adoptees, and other out-groups.

Immigrants, including Bangladeshi laborers and Vietnamese mail-order brides, now constitute two percent of South Korea's population, a number that is climbing rapidly. A significant number of marriages now involve a foreign spouse, usually a woman from Southeast Asia. It's not unusual to find oneself surrounded by foreigners on Seoul's buses and subways. But rampant xenophobia still lurks under the surface.

Jasmine Bacurnay Lee was born in the Philippines in 1977, married a Korean sailor, emigrated to the ROK in 1995, and eventually became a popular television personality and women's rights advocate. In April 2012, she became the first non-ethnic Korean elected to the South Korean National Assembly. It's interesting to compare her story to that of Fleur Pellerin, who was abandoned on the streets of Seoul as an infant in 1973, adopted by French parents, and in May 2012, was appointed by President Francois Hollande as France's first Korean-born minister (for the digital economy). Pellerin denies that racial prejudice was an obstacle to her political ascent. But Lee's unique success has much to do with her good looks and fame. After her election, anti-immigration activists called for her expulsion on the grounds that "poisonous weeds from abroad are corrupting the Korean bloodline."

For Koreans, ethnic xenophobia is often tinged with class prejudice. I once knew a Korean American guy who was sexually retarded. He had always followed his parents' stern guidelines to study hard and avoid dating until after he finished medical school. He dutifully complied. But then at the age of twenty-eight, he fell in love with an Irish nurse. When he told his parents he wanted to marry this white woman, they disowned him. They told him that it wasn't her race but her occupation, which they believed was beneath him. A few years later, he broke up with her, and announced his engagement to an English scientist who was even more educated then himself. His parents grudgingly acquiesced.

Asian parents often admonish their children for taking an interest in people of lower social standing; they expect them to marry up. This lack of compassion led to many lower-class children being abandoned in the first several decades following the Korean War. Many of these so-called "orphans" actually had parents who would have taken care of them had they received more support than their impoverished extended families could provide. But today, most abandoned children don't come from poor families; they come from single mothers. This brings us to the last and largest out-group of all: women.

Ibyang Munje

Let's take another, closer look at the issue of Korean adoption (*ibyang munje*). South Korea now has one of the lowest birth rates in the developed world, a dwindling indigenous workforce necessitating an influx of foreign labor, and an aging population that needs more young people to take care of them. Yet thousands of healthy Korean children are abandoned each year. What's going on? We can begin to understand this paradox by analyzing the demographics of adoptees and their birth mothers over the last 70 years. The *ibyang munje* surprisingly encapsulates the full panoply of Korean intolerance.

In the immediate aftermath of the Korean War, most adoptees were either orphans or the half-breed progeny of American soldiers. Too destitute to take care of the former and too racist to deal compassionately with the latter, Syngman Rhee's fledgling government gladly handed the poor waifs to paternalistic Americans. At the time, many people in the United States sincerely believed it their God-given duty to save the Yellow race from themselves. The wheels of adoption were set in motion by the combination of American idealism and Korean desperation.

By the 1970's, with wartime memories fast fading and most of the first generation of half-breeds gone, the prejudice had shifted from race to class. The adoptee demographic was now dominated by little girls born in poverty. This coincided with President Park's push for industrialization at all costs. Precious resources were not to be wasted helping poor farmers raise more daughters. Park wanted to limit the growth of the rural population (through emigration, abortion, and adoption) and get more men to work in the shipyards. But where there's a supply and a demand, there's money to be made. According to Professor Eleana Kim, author of *Adopted Territory*, "in addition to functioning as a mechanism of population control and securing national loyalty through state racism, adoption became a source of foreign capital early during the postwar reconstruction. It could well be argued that orphanages (which were largely funded by Western relief organizations), and, later, state-subsidized adoption agencies, functioned as a surrogate welfare system and a conduit for foreign exchange." As many critics cynically pointed out during the 1988 Seoul Olympics, Korea's most lucrative export was its children, a fact not lost on the North Korean ministry of propaganda.

Finally, starting in the 1990's, the demographics changed once again: roughly equal numbers of boys and girls born to a mix of lower and middle class single mothers. To explain this final shift, one needs to understand the misogynistic bent of Korean neo-Confucianism. Starting in the seventeenth century, the aristocratic (*yangban*) class of the Yi Dynasty decided to favor agnatic kinship (descent through the paternal line) and institutionalized primogeniture. Things haven't changed much since.

As Eleana Kim notes, "prior to the seventeenth century, women, wives' relatives, and nonkin adoptees could have inheritance rights. With the ascendance of primogeniture, agnatic adoptions became the norm and women's status was reduced through their exclusion from ancestral rites and inheritance. A woman's value became wholly dependent upon her ability to bear a son for her husband's lineage." This explains why until recently, poor women in Korea (and China) chose to abort or abandon their daughters and try again for a son.

Modern Korea is a rich nation, where most families can afford to raise daughters as well as sons. The problem now is another historical legacy of neo-Confucian morality: the stigma attached to single motherhood. Because the family name is passed down through the paternal line, a child of an unwed mother is simply undesirable for any man other than the father. It is a disgrace for an unmarried woman to give birth and an embarrassment for a man to adopt her children. Women are under pressure to get married first and then bare children for her husband, preferably boys. But accidents happen. Girls get pregnant, couples break up, fathers die. Being a single mother in Western Europe or the United States is never easy, but they usually get by with support from family and the state. There's no particular shame in being a single mother or in marrying one. Not so in Korea. Single mothers are routinely ostracized by coworkers, neighbors, and even their own families. People feel pressure not to hire them or to befriend them. There are frequent reports of fathers disowning their daughters. What makes it particularly worse is that the state reinforces this intolerance by failing to support single mothers. Unfortunately for many women, the pressure to give up their children is enormous.

In the United States, nearly 40 percent of children are now born out of wedlock. In South Korea, that figure is less than 2 percent. This reflects the strength of Asian family values. Nearly all unmarried women in Korea terminate their pregnancies, but of the ones that are carried to term, *nearly three-quarters* are given up for adoption. In America, that figure is about 1 percent. This reflects something else entirely: Koreans' intolerance for the reproductive choices of pregnant women. As the journalist Choe Sang-hun wrote in the New York Times (Oct 8, 2009), "each year, social pressure drives thousands of unmarried women to choose between abortion, which is illegal but rampant, and adoption, which is considered socially shameful but is encouraged by the government. The few women who decide to raise a child alone risk a life of poverty and disgrace." The chief reason why so many young Korean women are giving up their children today is not because they are poor, but because they live in a sexist society. Yet the *ibyang munje* is a complex one. The confluence of medieval neo-Confucian misogyny, *danil minjok*-inspired outgroup hostility, an American savior mentality, and the commodification of children in the global adoption supermarket have conspired to create 160,000 lost souls.

A particularly tragic case, also reported by Choe Sang-hun in the New York Times (July 2, 2017) is the life and death of Phillip Clay. Born Kim Sang-pil in 1975, he was abandoned in Seoul at age 6 and picked up by the Holt agency. His first American family gave him up after a year, and a second family, the Clays, adopted him in 1983. Things did not go well for Phillip over the subsequent three decades. Suffering from bipolar disorder, substance abuse, and alcoholism, he became estranged from his adoptive parents, and suffered a string of arrests on burglary and drug-related charges. Because his father never bothered to fill out the paperwork necessary to obtain United States citizenship for him, Philip was eventually deported to South Korea in 2012. That's when things got even worse. Unable to speak the language, and having no one to help him navigate the culture, Phillip became jobless, homeless, and destitute. His mental disorder worsened and he attempted to take his life by ingesting paint thinner. He was hospitalized, but was unable to find an outpatient clinic with an English-speaking staff. His lack of fluency in Korean combined with the stigma of mental illness virtually guaranteed long-term unemployment. Phillip finally ended his life by leaping from the 14th floor of an apartment building in Seoul. He was 42 years old. Phillip was caught in a perfect storm at the very heart of Korean culture. What really killed him was the fact that Koreans stigmatize single mothers, the mentally ill, and ethnic Koreans ignorant of their culture. And the reason why Koreans stigmatize them lies at the historical intersection of neo-Confucian conservatism and ethnic nationalism.

Expanding Circles

South Koreans may not be starving in forced labor camps or terrorized by the thought police like their northern cousins, but their society is deeply fractured in other ways. Racism, sexism, and classism are rampant. Foreigners and biracial children are treated badly. Some Koreans think modern society is to blame and that the solution is to embrace traditional Confucian values even more tightly. Old-fashioned Confucian academies (*seowon*) designed to inculcate a deeper respect for elders and teach etiquette are making a comeback. But the flip side of respect and obedience is domination and coercion. What Korea really needs is a responsible liberal welfare state. The nation may have entered the twenty-first century economically and technologically, but it is mired in the nineteenth century socially. Their culture emphasizes conservative ideals that may have held the society together during the days of the Japanese Empire, but they don't promote wellbeing today.

The philosopher Peter Singer has proposed the notion of the *moral circle*. In prehistoric times, people applied their moral intuition to the small bands and tribes in which they lived and loved. All others were members of the out-group, to which empathy and fairness did not apply. As societies gradually evolved into cities, states, and nations, the moral circle expanded accordingly. Today, people routinely pledge allegiance to nation states, ethnicities, and religions comprising hundreds of millions of individuals. A liberal minority even expresses loyalty to the brotherhood of all humankind and even to some of the more human-like species now threatened with extinction. Koreans would do well to study Peter Singer and apply his moral circle to their own narrow prejudices.

6

What's Happenin' Hotstuff?
Sex & the Angry Asian Man

> Women everywhere in all times have been more vulnerable than men. They've been held down and kept down, and have suffered immeasurably more at the hands of their opposites. This is true of women of the East and Eastern women in the West. But I also believe that, in certain spheres of life in twenty-first-century America, Asian women have it better than Asian men.
>
> Alex Tizon
> *Big Little Man*

> I'm an Asian girl. I don't date Asian guys. Yep, I'm one of those that date lots and lots of (mostly, but not always) white guys. Why? It's simple: I'm a racist.
>
> Jenny An
> *XOJane*

Kevin is an angry Asian man. He's angry that at 30, he's still living with his mother, who expects devotion from her "golden child". He's angry with his dead-end job at the bank, where he hasn't been promoted in a decade. He's angry about his mediocre performance in school, a fact his family is too ashamed to acknowledge. He's angry at the attention granted to his more successful cousins and siblings who are now dentists and doctors. But mostly he's angry that he's never had a girlfriend. Kevin always fantasized about going out with beautiful (usually white) women, but aside from a few abortive attempts in college, he's never had the nerve to try. He is convinced women find him ridiculous. Physically, he's a bit short (about 5'4"), wears oversize glasses, sports out of style T-shirts and ill-fitting jeans, and is in need of a good haircut, but he's not otherwise ugly. When not running errands for his mother, he spends his hours playing video games and watching ESPN, where he imagines himself playing for the NBA Championships and attracting scores of nubile fans of the feminine persuasion.

Kevin is neither mentally ill nor sociopathic. He just happens to be one of the millions of Asian American men who don't neatly fit the model minority myth. These men face the dual and often incompatible pressures of living up to the expectations of the Asian family while simultaneously trying to overcome the negative stereotypes of the Asian American man. Trying to succeed at both, they often end up achieving neither. The resulting loss of self-confidence takes its toll, making further failure inevitable. Some self-destruct in bitter frustration. But most trudge on in silent desperation. This chapter is about them.

AM seeking WF

When I walk the streets in New York City (or any other metropolitan area, for that matter), I see many more Asian women in the hands of white men than the other way round. When I'm with my wife, who is white, I make it a game to see how many more Asian woman/white man (AWWM) couples I can spot compared with Asian man/white woman (AMWW) couples. She thinks it's a bit pointless, but I find the results telling: the ratio of AWWM:AMWW is about three to one.

I've been aware of the gender-race discrepancy since my college days at MIT. Nearly a quarter of my class was Asian, and many classmates were in interracial relationships. They typically involved an Asian female and her white boyfriend. AMWW couples were rare. The few Asian boys with white girlfriends were often cocky types. One Chinese guy I knew loved to take his blond girlfriend to Asian parties just to show her off. Obnoxious as it was, the tactic worked: many of us viewed him with a mixture of envy and awe. For many years, I considered the attractive intellectual white woman the *sine qua non et magna cum laude* of sexual fulfillment. I never asked out an Asian girl and no white girl ever asked me out, so nothing ever happened. But I don't think attractive Asian girls would have been all that interested in me either. Many of them were too busy being courted by white boys.

Personal anecdotes make for poor statistical analysis. If we want to get to the truth behind the stereotypes, we'll need lots of data points. Sociology professor C.N. Le, director of the Asian and Asian American Studies Program at the University of Massachusetts, Amherst, runs a blog called *Asian Nation*, which aims to use "census data to analyze and compare socioeconomic and demographic outcomes of assimilation among Asian Americans." His research based on the 2010 census is revealing. In all the major immigrant groups from East and Southeast Asia (Chinese, Filipino, Japanese, Korean, and Vietnamese), the intermarriage rate with Caucasian men far exceeded that with Caucasian women. In fact, Asian women were more likely to marry non-Asian men across the board (including black, Hispanic, or mixed-race) than Asian men were to marry non-Asian women. In 2010, fifteen percent of Chinese American women were married to Caucasians and 0.3% were married to black men, but only five percent of Chinese American men were married to Caucasians and 0.1% were married to black women. [These results include all ethnic Chinese living in the United States. Not surprisingly, more assimilated Asian Americans have higher rates of interracial marriage than recent immigrants. But even if we correct for that, the three to one gender gap remains.] Among Korean Americans, twenty-five percent of women were married to white men and 1.4% to black men, but only five percent of Korean American men were married to Caucasian women and 0.2 to black women. The most ethnically mixed demographic belongs to Japanese Americans. But even here, while thirty-eight percent of women are married to white men and 2.1% to black men, only nineteen percent of men are married to whites and 0.2% married to blacks. Interestingly, this race-gender pattern does not exist among immigrants from the Indian subcontinent; only about four percent of both men and women in this demographic married Caucasians.

Most of my readers will agree that the term "Asian American", like "European American", applies to such a broad panoply of cultural, linguistic, and ethnic backgrounds that it's not terribly useful. Why should we lump so many different people together? The reason is that despite Asian American diversity, there is a persistent interracial gender gap in mate selection regardless of national origin, socioeconomic status, or degree of assimilation. This is an observationally anomaly that simply needs an explanation. Why would an Asian man, whether a recent immigrant from Vietnam, a fourth-generation Japanese American, or an adopted Korean orphan, be less likely to marry outside his race than his matching female counterpart? Is it because he doesn't want to or because he can't?

The problem has two components: race and sex. As I pointed out in the second chapter, human racial differences evolved relatively recently (within the last 100,000 years) and are thus biologically much less significant than sexual differences, which have been around as long as complex life existed on the planet (more than 600,000,000 years). So before we can answer the question of why Asian American men and women differ in their mating outcomes, we need to ask a more general question about gender differences.

A Brief History of Sex

What's the point of sex? In the Sisyphean struggle against the second law of thermodynamics commonly known as *life on earth*, living bodies follow two fundamental imperatives: procure energy to live on, and reproduce before you die. In this line of reasoning, simple creatures like viruses and protozoa, thanks to their tiny size and vast numbers, have an inherent advantage over larger ones. They are much more efficient in extracting resources, often through parasitization of larger hosts. Large creatures have responded by evolving formidable defenses including woody bark, hard shells, mucous membranes, and immune systems. But the parasites have yet another advantage: their phenomenal rates of reproduction (sometimes several times an hour) allow them to evolve countermeasures more rapidly than their hosts. No matter how elaborate the host defense, given enough time, the pathogens will eventually evolve a way to infiltrate it. This is precisely how bacteria become antibiotic resistant and tumors become chemotherapy resistant.

The solution is to change the codes (the genes) for the locks (the proteins that make up the immune response) rapidly enough to keep a step ahead of the parasites. There are two ways to do this. One is through the natural selection of random mutations. Even in organisms that reproduce by parthenogenesis, mutations naturally accrue over scores of generations. A tiny fraction of them will turn out to be advantageous, by chance. But as a tactic for dealing with bacteria that have a doubling time of several hours, luck is simply too slow to rely upon; lock-picking microorganisms mutate much faster, outsmarting host defenses before they have a chance to be upgraded. A better approach is to shuffle your offspring's genes at each generation by exchanging your DNA with that of someone else. Now that is the point of sex.

Sex was invented as a response to infectious disease. Bacteria can afford the quick and dirty approach of asexual reproduction (although they too occasionally engage in a kind of sexual intercourse called *conjugation*). Single celled eukaryotes like amoeba and yeast are often parasitized themselves, so most of them engage in both sexual and asexual reproduction, depending on environmental conditions. Sex gets complicated with true multicellular organisms. We are talking about creatures with billions of differentiated cells. Producing offspring requires a dedicated set of undifferentiated stem cells. Many plants and some higher animals can reproduce asexually simply by allowing their stem cells to develop into unfertilized embryos which will grow up as clones of their parent. But virgin birth is not ideal. Sex provides variety in terms of locks and keys, and that prevents infection. No sex, no diversity. No diversity, more parasites.

The trick is to produce germ cells (unfertilized stem cells) that don't spontaneously self-fertilize within one's own body, because that would defeat the whole purpose of sexual exchange. Higher organisms accomplish this by differentiating and segregating their germ cells so that only different types can fuse into a viable zygote. In theory, many kinds of germ cells could have evolved, but it is much more economical to have just two. One became compact, mobile, and stripped down to no more than its packet of genes, some mitochondria, and a powerful flagellum. They are cheap and abundant. The other grew big, stationary, and bloated with the nutrients and building blocks needed to nurture a new embryo. They are much more expensive to make. The gender wars had begun.

Reproductive Economics

Plants and some lower animals, like hermaphroditic nematode worms, are able to produce both sets of germ cells. For these species, sex differences exist in the germ cells but not in their parents. But most animals have opted for a division of labor in which the production of germ cells also requires the sexual differentiation of the bodies making them. Only females can produce eggs, and only males can produce sperm. This is where things get interesting. As I noted earlier, sperm and egg are not identical. Although both contribute equally to the genetic make-up of the offspring, the environmental cost is greatly skewed towards the female germ cell. Because it takes so much effort to prepare eggs, the body who makes them usually has a much greater stake in their development. In other words, the evolution of sex differentiation was driven by the economics of reproduction.

In economics, it makes sense for the seller of an expensive commodity to hold out for the best deal, while the hawker of a cheapo brand should unload it whenever possible. So it is with the economics of sex. The few seeming exceptions actually prove the rule. With some species, such as the Panamanian poison arrow frog and the *Chicana bird* of South America, there is a reversal of the traditional sex role. The males do the hard work of incubating the eggs. This more than makes up for the cost females put into making them. In such cases, one would expect females to compete for sexual access to choosey males. This is in fact what happens. But with most mammals, and almost all primates, females make the greater reproductive investment. Here, the expense of making eggs is compounded by the added cost of gestation, the risk of childbirth, and the effort of nursing, none of which are borne by the male. With so little to invest, it makes sense for males to play the field.

The rules of the game, which vary from species to species depending on environmental circumstance, have left indelible marks on morphology and physiology. The comparative anatomy of the great apes gives us a fascinating window onto the evolution of primate sexual behavior. The male mountain gorilla is a giant beast, twice the size of its female companion. But his testicles are relatively small, in proportion to body weight, compared with those of the chimpanzee. The male chimpanzee is only a bit larger than the female, and the highly promiscuous African pigmy chimpanzee, or *bonobo*, shows no sexual dimorphism at all. Yet all chimps have enormous testicles. This makes sense in light of reproductive behavior. Gorillas live in isolated pockets of rain forest in the highlands of Congo. Solitary males compete to dominate a territory that includes a harem of females. Once on top, the alpha male enjoys a sexual monopoly. He can rest assured that all the offspring in his territory are his without having to engage in repeated intercourse just to make sure. There was selective pressure to be big and strong, but not necessarily to have big balls.

Chimps, in contrast, live in large social groups constantly interacting with males and females from neighboring communities. Unlike gorillas, both sexes are organized hierarchically, and it is much more difficult for single males to dominate females. The alpha males and females got there not by being physically imposing but by being socially adroit. So selection favored brains over size. And because females are promiscuous, a male of any rank cannot be sure whose baby is his. So it pays to have lots of sex, hence the large testicles.

Finally, in the gibbon species, males and females are the same size, and the males have small testes. This is consistent with the fact that gibbons are solitary creatures that roam large areas of forest without running into others. Males don't compete much and couples mate for life.

Where do we fit in? In terms of sexual dimorphism and testicle size, humans lie between gorillas and chimpanzees. Men are about fifteen percent larger than women, and their testicles are twice the size of the gorilla's but half the size of the chimpanzee's. This implies that our male ancestors did not fight to monopolize groups of females as much as gorillas, nor were they as promiscuous as chimpanzees, but neither were they as peaceful or monogamous as the gibbon.

What Women Want

The inherent biological inequality in reproductive investment is the reason that men and women have evolved differing mating strategies. It is also the source of much conflict and bloodshed, both between and within the sexes. But humans are complex thinking creatures. Our behavior cannot be reduced to tidy genetic algorithms or accurately predicted by studying the mating habits of African primates. Evolutionary biology and comparative ethnography offer only a rough guide to the human condition. What are women and men really like and whom do they like? What do they look for in short and long term partners?

As noted earlier, the most important things in life are feeding and fucking. In our ancestral history, the sexes had unequal access to these resources. Males, being larger and stronger, were natural hunters. They could provide the calories essential for the group's survival in times of famine. Females were the gatekeepers to reproduction. Without their consent, the species would go extinct. This sets up a natural trade-off. Women need resources, men need sex. But, as the evolutionary psychologist David Buss writes in his book, *The Evolution of Desire*, "those who hold valuable resources do not give them away cheaply or unselectively. Because women in our evolutionary past risked enormous investment as a consequence of having sex, evolution favored women who were highly selective about their mates."

In the 1990's, Buss conducted a landmark survey on the sexual preferences and attitudes of over 10,000 people all over the world. Both sexes rated kindness and compatibility equally high on the list of qualities they found attractive in a sexual partner. But they differed on others like wealth and social status. Women want men with resources. Every year, the men whom women marry earn more than men of the same age whom women do not marry. Especially alluring were men who lavished expensive gifts like jewelry and designer clothes, because this signals the man's willingness to part with resources the woman finds valuable. This is why rich old men like Rupert Murdoch and Donald Trump find it so easy to attract beautiful young women. In contrast, men are often too intimidated to date women with superior economic capacity. Moreover, women who earn more than their husbands seek divorce at twice the rate of women whose husbands earn more than they do.

One counterargument is that women have traditionally been poorer than men, and that seeking a wealthy partner is a utilitarian necessity rather than a matter of sexual attraction. But this would predict that wealthy or powerful women should be equally attracted to rich and poor men, and they are not. David Buss found that female CEOs of major corporations usually insisted on partners who were even richer or more powerful than they were. Wealth and social status are important to women in all cultures, regardless of religious background, political inclination, or socioeconomic standing because it implies the ability to provide resources for their children. The preference is so hardwired into the female brain that it stands even if the woman is wealthy or childless.

Confidence and assertiveness also rank high on the list. They signal the man's potential position in the social hierarchy and his ability to defend his commitments. Men who are dominant in their approach to women have a significant advantage over those who are passive because women have evolved to prefer mates who can provide protection as well as resources. What good is a generous partner if he is likely to be killed off by his competitors? An outgoing, through not overly aggressive, approach tells the woman that this guy is no pushover. Confidence doesn't necessarily mean the man has his partner's best interests in mind, but it improves the odds that he can deliver what he promises. Assertive women, on the other hand, are not particularly attractive to men because they present a potential challenge to his leadership. Sex is what women have and men want. When a woman has the upper hand, the man tends to get less of it.

This brings us to physical size and strength. Height implies strength, another quality women find attractive. Taller men get more responses on dating sites, are more popular in school, are promoted more often, and are more likely to win elections than shorter men. All things being equal, women consistently prefer to date men who are taller than average, and certainly taller than they are. This puts tall women at a disadvantage, because they still insist on dating even taller men, reducing their pool of prospective mates. The selective pressure largely explains why men are on average two to four inches taller than their mates in every culture and population.

Height, strength, and athleticism are desirable because, like assertiveness, they signal the male's ability to protect his mate, especially when she is pregnant or nursing. A strong bodyguard is often the best defense against other hostile males. Additionally, unlike wealth or status, they are *fitness indicators*: signs that the man has good genes which he can pass on to his partner's children. The "quality" of a gene is dependent on context. While some mutations are downright detrimental to health, most have subtle effects that depend on their interactions with other genes and with the environment. Figuring out what a given gene will do for an individual is notoriously difficult to predict even for scientists armed with the latest generation DNA sequencer. But a remarkably large number of physical and psychological traits are heritable, a fact that was not lost on our female ancestors. They may not have had the tools of the modern molecular geneticist, but they had something more powerful: an eye for genetic gestalt. By selecting men who are taller and stronger, a woman increases the likelihood that her sons will grow up to be more desirable to their potential mates, which, in turn, is advantageous for her own genes.

Sexual selection for fitness indicators is responsible for much of the tremendous variability in the animal kingdom, including, for instance, the seeming paradox of the *Marvelous Spatuletail hummingbird*. Extravagant male displays that are costly and even dangerous to maintain could not be the product of natural selection. But they may reveal something positive in the underlying genetic background: it takes robust health to build brilliant plumage, or rippling muscles, or lanky limbs. When females evolved to discriminate and select mates based on expensive fitness indicators, males competed to develop more of them. Both sexes choose mates based on fitness indicators, but because females invest more in their offspring, they have a greater incentive to be selective. Generally, men want to have many children, but women want the best children. In the trade off between quantity and quality, sexual selection became a bigger tool for females and may have driven the evolution of many uniquely male characteristics.

The interesting thing about sexual selection is that it tends to produce traits that are unnecessary or even harmful. An inclination to take sensible risks, for instance, is useful in moderation and one can imagine females favoring males who possess the trait. They can't know which genes are responsible for risk-taking, so they select mates whose behavior or appearance indicates that they have them. Males respond by competing with one another in ever more reckless displays of showmanship, hoping to impress females. Males evolve to become daredevils because females evolve to find daredevils sexy, which, in turn, makes males even more daring. Eventually this arms race reaches a steady state in which the greatest daredevils are likely to kill themselves in motorcycle accidents and gang wars before they have a chance to mate, but the most timid risk takers are likely to be passed up by choosy females and end up in reproductive oblivion. A trait that started off as a fitness indicator becomes decoupled from its original utility, and develops its own dynamic. This is known as *runaway selection.*

The male propensity for risk-taking coupled with their need to compete for female attention has resulted in the shortened male lifespan. Women outlive men by about five years in large part because males are much more likely to succumb to accidents, homicide, and suicide. Young men in their twenties suffer a mortality rate twice that of women their age. But there are advantages. Males seem to have a broader fitness curve. They may be the more vulnerable sex in terms of general health, longevity, and rates of developmental disability. Yet at the far right tail of the bell curve, the best and brightest also tend to be men. Not all of this can be explained by social and cultural factors. This again may be a consequence of female sexual selection working to broaden the male fitness spread.

This brings us to intelligence. The best way for a man to pick up a cute girl at a singles' club is to be witty. Stand up comedy ain't easy. It takes a fair amount of mental agility (and courage) to come up with good lines and quick retorts with strangers in a noisy bar. A nimble wit is at once a window to a man's mind and a fitness indicator of his genes. It tells a woman that this man is clever, and can probably outwit lesser rivals in competition for resources. It subconsciously signals that his (and hopefully her) sons will also probably be clever and therefore equally attractive to potential future girlfriends. This is why women find witty men sexy and why many men have evolved to be so ridiculously witty. But over the course of human history, runaway selection for wit has developed a logic quite divorced from any survival skills. The genes for wit are also the genes for working memory and cognitive capacity. Selecting mates based on these indicators increases the general intelligence of the population. Women also get big brains because these genes end up in both sexes. In his book, *The Mating Mind*, evolutionary psychologist Geoffrey Miller goes so far as to say that runaway sexual selection has led directly to the evolution of the oversize human brain which men then use to compose moonlight sonatas and love sonnets. This is all rather speculative. Another explanation is that these are just *spandrels* (phenotypic characteristics that are the by-product of the evolution of something else). Blood is red not because it was selected for its color, but because its oxygen carrying capacity requires hemoglobin, which happens to be red. Similarly, perhaps art, music, and literature are, in the words of Steven Pinker, "mental cheesecakes" made by brains that evolved to do something else.

Tall, witty, confident types who drive fancy cars and dole out expensive gifts are more likely to talk the girl out of her panties that first night. But then what? Immediate resources and good genes are important for young women who want to have children, but they're not so useful if her mate leaves her. Also, wealth and status take a long time to accrue; the most powerful men are often old and infirm. Women tend to marry men who are three to five years older because they are slightly more mature and accomplished than those their own age, but if a woman waits twenty years, her husband may soon end up dead. So females need to be sensitive to male characteristics that signal future dependability. These include ambition, stability, and commitment.

Not all men are equally productive over time. A 25 year-old medical student may be poorer than a 25 year-old nightclub promoter, but that is likely to change. Women looking for long-term partners find behaviors that reflect future success, such as diligence and ambition, more attractive than profligacy. It is also not lost on them that ostentatious men tend to attract other women. These men may be easier to bed than to keep around. In the market for the ideal husband, the ambitious nerd has his advantages.

Mental stability is another important trait to have in a potential marriage partner. It pays for a man to be impulsive early in the courtship process; surprise gifts and last minute vacations are surefire ways to attract females. But once the excitement wears off, most women do not prefer constant unpredictability. It reflects poor self-control and a lack of discipline. Walter Mischel's classic marshmallow experiment demonstrated that impulsive children are more likely to end up obese, diseased, and poor as adults compared to those who are more inhibited. A long-term relationship with an emotionally unstable man is costly, both in terms of lost resources and psychological well-being. Self-control has a strong genetic component, and not surprisingly, women use it as a fitness indicator. So women have evolved to be receptive to cautious, thoughtful men even while they expect gifts and surprises from them early on.

There is some truth to the old adage: "men put up with love to get sex, and women put up with sex to get love." Most women prefer a single committed lover over a long line of conquests. And the best indicator of future commitment is past commitment. Men who were promiscuous in the past are more likely to be unfaithful in the future. All things being equal, it makes sense for women in the marriage market to be more receptive to men who have had fewer sexual partners. But of course, things are never equal. Less experienced men usually have less experience not because they were romantically holding out for their one and only, but because they failed to impress as many women.

Women have what men want; it is in their power to grant men sexual access to their bodies in the short term. This allows them to pick and choose the best amongst their suitors. But when it comes to long-term commitment, the tables are turned. It is more in the female's interest to enter into marriage. Now her boyfriend has the upper hand. He can be choosier in picking a wife. The irony is that the men whom women attract tend to be of a higher quality in resources and in fitness than those they end up marrying, while the women that men choose to marry are superior (in their mind) to those they simply date. If this theory holds true, it would predict that men marry up, while women marry down. This sets up a delicate conundrum for a woman. Her husband, no matter how committed, may not be the best source of genes for her progeny. This is the reason why many otherwise happily married women consent to affairs. Men cheat for themselves; women cheat for their unborn children.

Once married with children, both parties have an investment in staying together. Men and women want kindness and affection from their partner, and rank them at the top of attractive qualities in the opposite sex because they are strong signals of commitment. But from an evolutionary standpoint, commitment is a compromise; neither sex is able to maximize its genetic potential through monogamy, but the alternatives are more likely to fail through intersexual conflict. This explains why strict monogamy is not the natural way of the world.

What Men Want

This brings us to what men want. The sexual investment theory predicts that men should be less choosy than women in their choice of mate. In David Lynch's film noir, *Blue Velvet*, the psychotic Frank Booth, played by Dennis Hopper, says, "I'll fuck anything that moves!" Some men probably would, but most of us are a bit more selective. But the selectivity is overwhelmingly physical. In every society throughout the world, men rank the physical attractiveness of a potential partner higher in importance than women do. Men consistently use the words pretty, lovely, gorgeous, beautiful, and ravishing to complement women; women rarely reciprocate in kind, and when they do, men usually take it as an insult to their masculinity. When the anthropologist Napoleon Chagnon asked Yanomamö men of Amazonia to describe the most attractive women, they insistently replied *moko dude*, referring to perfectly ripe fruit. Men have evolved to maximize their reproductive success, and the best way to ensure this is to mate with the most fertile females.

Female reproductive physiology is the rate-limiting step in human procreation. Women ovulate just once a month, carry at most three or four fetuses for nine months, nurse for several more years, and are menopausal by fifty. Historically, the narrow window of fertility forced men to compete for the youngest girls able to bear children, usually 13 to 15 years of age. But not all girls are equally fecund. Other physiological factors such as percentage and distribution of body fat, estrogen and androgen levels, nutrition, and the presence of infectious diseases all affect a young woman's likelihood of bearing healthy children. Not surprisingly, the male brain has evolved a preference for signs that indicate reproductive fitness. These include a 0.7 waist to hip ratio, well developed breasts, good teeth and nails, clear skin, and long hair (which indicates a prolonged period of good health and hygiene). Also important is facial symmetry and *neoteny*, the retention of juvenile traits into adulthood. The most distinctive facial characteristics of the adult male are the growth of facial hair and the heavy brow ridge, both of which develop as a result of exposure to androgens during puberty. Females who produce abnormally high levels of androgens develop similar characteristics and are also less fertile. So males naturally find women with delicate faces and bone structure attractive, and those with coarse features and moustaches repulsive.

Neoteny serves another purpose: it potentiates male dominance. As we have seen, thousands of rounds of male competition for females have resulted in significant sexual dimorphism. Men are, on average, larger, stronger, and more aggressive than females. Women, on average, are smaller and look more delicate than males. Larger and taller men also tend to be more confident than smaller men and this further enhances their rate of success in the dating game. Smaller men are more likely to be intimidated by larger, more imposing women. So just as being tall opens up more possibilities for men, appearing small opens up more possibilities for women. By appearing more fragile than she really may be, a woman is sending a signal of reassurance to an otherwise desirable male, stroking his ego enough for him to want to commit his resources. This is why delicacy is associated with femininity: it broadens a woman's appeal to a wider male audience.

Healthy young women with full figures and delicate faces have a selective advantage over women who do not have these traits, and men have been naturally selected to find them "beautiful". But as was the case with runaway female selection for male intelligence and aggression, things have a way of quickly getting out of hand. Most healthy women are equally fertile. You don't have to be a Victoria's Secret model to get a reproductive advantage. In fact, these women tend to be *less fertile*, given their anorexic diets and addictive habits. But the male attraction to certain feminine traits rooted in reproductive physiology has been co-opted by the male competition for status, which, in turn, drives female competition to artificially enhance those traits. Men can enhance their social standing among their peers by attracting "beautiful" women. When an otherwise attractive man is seen with an unattractive partner, he suffers a precipitous fall in his reputation and status. Meanwhile, the unattractive woman does not become more attractive because she is now with an attractive man. In contrast, when a beautiful woman goes out with a physically ugly man, his reputation soars, while she still remains beautiful. So important is the effect of feminine beauty on the male ego that attracting trophy wives has become an end in itself, quite divorced from any utility it might have for procreation. Men compete fiercely to attract the most beautiful women, and women respond by competing fiercely to look more beautiful. To see the pervasive effect of this arms race, just look at every ad in any woman's magazine.

It is a well-known fact that men are easily aroused merely by the mere thought of anonymous sex. In an amusing experiment, the psychologists R.

D. Clark and Elaine Hatfield hired attractive men and women to approach random college students and ask them out on a date, invite them to their dorm room, or offer to engage in sex. Half the male and female subjects agreed to a date. However, while none of the women consented to sex, seventy-five percent of the men did so, and the rest were apologetic but hardly offended. Compared to women, men tend to lose sexual interest in their long-term partners faster, but their libidos are much more likely to be rekindled by the prospect of a new partner. Men also tend to be much more receptive to sexual imagery, which, of course, fuels the pornography industry. The evolutionary psychologist Donald Symonds wrote, "the waning of lust for one's wife is adaptive...because it promotes a wandering eye." Variety is said to be the spice of life, and this is no less true of the male sexual appetite. Many men consider women from exotic backgrounds especially erotic for this reason.

This brings us to promiscuity. In the words of Alfred Kinsey: "There seems to be no question but that the human male would be promiscuous in his choice of sexual partners throughout the whole of his life if there were no social restrictions." Homosexual men, who don't face the social restrictions imposed by the traditional institution of marriage, are generally much more promiscuous then heterosexual men. In this sense, the contrast is not so much between gay and straight men, who both want casual sex, but between men and women, who don't. Casual sex has been an adaptive male reproductive strategy for millions of years, and its legacy can be found in the much greater male propensity to rush a date to bed, patronize prostitutes, purchase pornography, and engage in incest. But these activities invariably lead to conflict with spouses, authorities, and one's own conscience. It takes two to tango. This is why men looking for casual sex prefer promiscuous women. As Mae West once reportedly said, "Men like women with a past because they hope history will repeat itself."

The beautifully seductive sex goddess is every man's fantasy. What's not to like? He gets easy sex with someone who may have his child, and better yet, if she marries someone else, that cuckold can help raise it. The problem comes when he decides he wants to marry her. For men, the greatest danger is a wife who carries another man's child. For women, it is a long-term partner who fails to deliver promised resources. These different reasons to fear betrayal lead to an interesting psychological gender mismatch. As Steven Pinker puts it: "men may be upset about affection because it could lead to sex; women may be upset about sex because it could lead to affection." When a woman cheats on her long-term partner, he risks not only losing his own genetic investment but also spending his hard won resources on the care of another man's child. So men have developed two defenses: marriage and jealousy. Jealousy is a primitive emotion triggered by the fear of losing access to a mate's resources. Men seem to experience it most intensely when they suspect their partner of sexual infidelity. It motivates them to guard their mate vigilantly, but sometimes backfires into self-destructive homicidal rages. The institution of marriage was invented as a way to legitimize commitment in a long-term relationship. But, in many societies, it simply allows a man to monopolize sexual access to his wife without reciprocating in kind. Jealousy in marriage is often detrimental to women because it reflects the male fear of female sexual independence.

Men want it both ways: a shameless slut for casual sex and a coy virgin for marriage. The Madonna-whore complex has insinuated itself into the schizophrenic nature of American popular culture with examples like Britney Spears ("I'm not a girl, not yet a woman"), and, well, Madonna ("Like a virgin"). Women are well aware of this unrealistic expectation, and, if they play their cards right, can trick men into thinking they can get two for one. So when it comes to marriage, the woman who is demure and devoted, at least in public, but sexually aggressive in the bedroom is most desirable because she can tickle both sides of the male sexual appetite.

The mating strategies of men and women diverge largely because the sexes are evolutionarily distinct; millions of years of selective pressure has left indelible marks on anatomy, physiology, and behavior. The differences amongst the human races, however, are much more subtle. Men and women are fundamentally different at a biological level in a way that Caucasians and Asians are not. This implies that Asian men and women have more in common with white men and white women, respectively, than they have with each other. But there are a few notable exceptions. With respect to East Asians, I will focus on three obvious distinguishing physical characteristics: stature, breasts, and eyes, before moving on to a highly sensitive topic for the Asian male: his penis.

Slants

On average, the people of East and Southeast Asia are indeed shorter than northern Europeans by about two to three inches. Mediterranean populations, such as Sicilians, also tend to be several inches shorter than those to their north, such as the Danes. This difference is at least partly genetic, possibly due to selection for the thermoregulatory advantage of small stature (increased body area to volume ratio) in warm, humid climates. But I can't help but notice that this relatively modest difference always seems to be exaggerated in war movies depicting hulking American soldiers decimating hapless hordes of diminutive Asians. Part of this reflects wartime stereotypes. But another reason is that in the last century, Caucasian Americans were actually better fed than East Asians. Note that South Koreans today are considerably taller than their malnourished northern cousins. With the homogenization of the global diet, size differences between the races are likely to diminish.

Biologists have recently begun to analyze racial differences using genome scans. One of the more interesting discoveries comes from Pardis Sabeti's lab at the Broad Institute of Harvard and MIT involving the *ectodysplasin* gene (EDAR). EDAR normally functions to regulate the embryonic development of connective tissue. Most Africans and Europeans have one version of the gene, but a majority of East Asians carry a different allele. Sabeti cloned this mutation and inserted it into mice. The resulting "knock-in" mice had thicker hair shafts, more sweat glands, and smaller mammary glands compared to controls. The mutant mice, in effect, developed "Asian traits".

The EDAR mutation is believed to have occurred thirty to thirty-five thousand years ago in central China and quickly spread throughout the Yangtze valley and beyond. Today, over two billion people carry this particular allele. Such rapid evolution points to a strong selective bias. What is unclear is whether the selection was natural or sexual, or some combination of the two. One can imagine that the pressure of living in a tropical climate, as central China was at the time, conferred a significant advantage to those who could sweat more efficiently. The EDAR mutants had this advantage, perhaps giving them a leg up in the competition for survival. The coarse straight hair and small breasts may simply have come along for the ride. However, they could also have functioned as fitness indicators, telling potential suitors of their genetic advantage. In time, sexual selection became a more potent means of spreading the mutation, as both sexes associated the EDAR phenotype with sexual attractiveness. The relatively small breasts of most Asian women may have been selected for this reason.

The single most distinctive facial characteristic amongst East Asians is the shape of their eyelids. As you might have expected, there is quite a bit of misinformation clouding the epicanthal fold. While prevalent throughout East and Southeast Asia, it is by no means universal. In addition, it is common amongst Central Asians and the Bushmen of southern Africa. And it has nothing to do with Down syndrome (once called "Mongoloid idiots"), mental retardation, or visual acuity. But stereotypes die hard and superficial features are the best vehicle for driving the racial insult. This is patently evident in the endless litany of caricatures and jokes involving "slitty" or "slanty" eyes. And, of course, the most common racist epithet for Asians as a group is *Chink*.

Like the small breast, the Asian eye is likely a byproduct of sexual selection. For some reason, ancient Asian women may have found young men with epicanthal folds irresistibly sexy and preferred to mate with them. But today, many Asian women, and even a few men, are having plastic surgery to make their eyes look more Western. The so-called "Asian blepharoplasty" is now the most common cosmetic surgical procedure performed on both East Asians and Asian Americans. I personally find this disturbing. The people who choose to have this procedure are, whether or not they admit it, self-hating Asians. It wouldn't be so bad if thousands of Western women underwent reverse blepheroplasty to look more Asian, but that is not the case. In their defense, many young Asian women claim that changing their appearance makes them more marketable in the dating and career market. There is probably some truth to this, but this only underscores the pervasive, and pernicious, influence of the Western beauty standard on the Asian psyche.

This brings us to the Asian penis. For such a fraught topic, surprisingly little objective research has been done. A study led by David Veale at

University College, London concludes that the "average" Asian male has an erect penis length of around five inches, which is about an inch shorter than that of Caucasian men and nearly two inches shorter than that of African men. In terms of methodology, selection, sample size, and measurement bias, studies like this are questionable. But the results do consistently indicate that Asians have smaller penises. This is not an interesting conclusion. Asian men are smaller and smaller men would be expected to have shorter penises in proportion. The interesting question would be: is the Asian penis *disproportionately* small, correcting for height? The only way to answer this conclusively is to gather a large number of young healthy men of various Asian, European, and African backgrounds, standardize them for age and height, and measure them repeatedly in a controlled setting. Getting funding for such a project may be even more difficult than for research on race and intelligence.

I propose that a field for legitimate further exploration is ethnic evolutionary and developmental endocrinology (EEDE?). Given their relatively sparse body hair, neotenous appearance, and lower rates of prostate cancer, men of East and Southeast Asian descent may have lower androgen activity. A handful of studies have been done comparing serum testosterone levels of various different ethnic groups. To date (2017), the results have not been statistically conclusive. But the researchers were looking at the wrong target. Androgens (testosterone and the related dihydrotestosterone, or *DHT*), like all sex hormones, exert powerful effects on metabolism and development indirectly through downstream interactions with their protein receptors and target genes. Most of these genes are transcription factors which themselves regulate dozens of other genes nestled within complex networks. Moreover, androgenic effects are not constant throughout the lifespan; they are much more profound during embryogenesis and again during puberty. So simply measuring serum testosterone levels in a group of adult men is an inadequate way to tell how much androgenic exposure they may have had over their lifetimes. It's like learning to cook by going out to a restaurant. Analyzing the finished product doesn't tell you how it got there. One would have to look at levels of prenatal testosterone, downstream enzymatic activity, and gene expression patterns in early life. For now, we can only make an educated guess based on androgenic markers such as secondary sexual characteristics. All that being said, however, I wouldn't be surprised if Asian populations are found to be less masculinized at a genetic level. Let good research speak for itself.

Too Shy Shy

In American society, there seems to be an unspoken stereotype that different races somehow fall along a sexual gradient. At one end of the spectrum are African Americans (of both sexes), who are considered the most masculine, followed by people of Hispanic, Middle Eastern and Southern European descent, Northern and Western Europeans, South Asians, and finally, East and Southeast Asians. Therefore, the reasoning goes, black men epitomize masculinity, and East Asian women embody femininity. There is far too much individual overlap to lend much scientific credence to this theory, but it does seem to affect dating and marriage patterns. It probably goes some way to explain why Asian women and black men are more likely to marry outside of their races than their opposite sex counterparts. Unfortunately, this leaves many Asian men and black women out of the mix. My wife suggests that sexually frustrated Asian men would do well to marry single black women. But this, of course, is the most unusual pairing of all.

It's now time to address the million-dollar question: why are Asian women more likely to date outside their race than Asian men? I will analyze the phenomenon from the perspective of its four characters: the white woman, the Asian man, the Asian woman, and the white man. Each has his or her reasons for attracting and rejecting those they do. According to J. T. Tran, self-professed Asian playboy and founder of a dating boot camp called *ABCs of Attraction*, the number one stereotype that white women have of Asian men is not that they have small penises or are wimpy computer hackers, but that they only date Asian women. If this is true, it is certainly not by choice. Plenty of Asian men fantasize about having glorious sex with beautiful women whose hair, as the journalist Wesley Yang wrote in his *New York Magazine* essay, "Paper Tigers", "is the color of the midday sun and eyes are the color of the ocean."

We have reviewed the traits women generally find attractive in a potential mate. Now let's see how Asian men stack up in the eyes of white women. I think there are four main reasons why this pairing is rare, and they all have to do with female choice. First is anatomy. Women may not care so much about penis size, but they are clearly selective about height. Asian men tend to be shorter, and so are more likely to be passed up. Secondly, women are attracted to witty men. But wit requires a mastery of the local language. English is a difficult second language for many foreign-born Asians. The third factor is culture. Most Asian children are raised by strict disciplinarians who expect them to sacrifice their social life to achieve educational excellence. Moreover, many immigrant parents pressure their sons to marry someone suitable within their own ethnic fold. Parental pressure combined with Confucian indoctrination of filial piety, self-denial, and modesty conspire to sabotage opportunities for interracial dating. Finally, there is psychology. Many Asian men have confidence issues, especially around Caucasian women they find attractive. This is the most complex and refractory of the four factors. Its proximate cause is the internalization of the Hollywood/media stereotype, but its ultimate roots lie even deeper in the Asian psyche.

Parental pressure to defer pleasure and cultural pressure against intermarriage affect Asian Americans of both sexes equally. But negative Hollywood stereotypes and the historic lack of positive media attention has disproportionately hurt the Asian male. Negative stereotypes tend to cause low self esteem, which makes Asian men less likely to ask white women out, but not for lack of interest. Hence the popularity of dating boot camps that preferentially cater to Asian men.

J.T. Tran made an interesting observation at a conference for Asian business students at the University of Pennsylvania's Wharton School. He said there are two different kinds of Asians that take his course: Asians born and raised in the U.S. and those who grew up overseas. The foreign Asians should be more inept. They tend to be even shorter than American-born Asians, their English is broken, their understanding of American culture is limited, they walk and dress the Asian way, and they're likely to have been raised in more conservative environments. But they often do better with white women than their more Americanized counterparts. How could this be? The answer is self-confidence.

The barriers of anatomy, language, and culture can be overcome. Asian men can work out and dress well to accentuate their physiques. In time, they can learn English. And with determination, they can reject the more restrictive elements of their culture and parental expectations. Women also tend to be more forgiving than many men realize. Many white women actually find Asian men physically attractive, find affinity with Asian family values, and will immerse themselves in Asian language and culture. Some years ago, one of my patients was a young attractive white woman who was so fascinated by Japanese anime that she quit her marketing job in New York and moved to Tokyo by herself.

Women come in all shapes and sizes, and their preferences in men come in all shapes and sizes. Small stature and lack of assertiveness may be drawbacks for some, but intelligence, diligence, and dependability are attractions for others. Since the qualities associated with Asian men are also those that women prefer in a long-term mate, one can make two interesting predictions: the Caucasian women Asian men date are likely to be older than those whom they don't, and white women are more likely to take Asian men as second husbands.

The big hurdle for Asian men is their psychology of avoidance. Women, no matter how receptive or open-minded, are not likely to approach a man who shows no outward sign of interest. How can she be expected to know that underneath his bashful exterior lurks a burning desire? The roots of Asian shyness lie deep in the Eastern cultural philosophy of passivity and collectivism I explored at length in the fourth chapter. It is so ingrained that many Asian men actually find it difficult to smile spontaneously. Back in college, I knew a white student who asked an Asian friend if he was mad. The friend replied that smiling actually made him feel ridiculous. In fairness, I knew plenty of other Asians who always seemed to smile for no particular reason.

The Asian poker face works well as a social lubricant in hierarchical collectivist societies like China, but fails in egalitarian individualistic societies like the United States. But old habits die hard, and many otherwise acculturated Asian Americans find it difficult to express themselves publicly. This leads to any number of cultural misunderstandings far beyond the dating scene. Highly qualified Asian Americans are routinely passed up for promotion because they don't speak up at board meetings, top students are rejected from selective colleges because they fail to liven up the interview, and, perhaps most damning of all, Hollywood and Madison Avenue continue their negative stereotyping because Asians tend not to complain. The roots of the bamboo ceiling grow from the soil of Asian passivity.

The bamboo ceiling is a self-propagating process. The more Asian Americans are kept out of the top rungs, the more of a blow it becomes to their self-esteem. Western stereotypes of Asians, largely propagated by Hollywood and media, play upon and magnify both biological and cultural characteristics. They make Asian men out to be small, effeminate, passive, nerdy buffoons: "what's happenin' hotstuff?" They make Asian women out to be promiscuous, docile, exotic, erotic sex kittens: "me love you long time!" These stereotypes, shaped by the attitudes and appetites of white consumers, have an insidious effect on second and third generation Asian Americans who internalize them simply because they are no longer Asian enough to have a cultural grounding to fall back on. For them, American culture **is** their culture, and it is a culture which tells them that they are small, effeminate, passive, nerdy buffoons who crash Molly Ringwald's Sweet Sixteen.

Loving the White Man

What about the preferences of the Asian woman? The comedian Dennis Hong recently did some unofficial research for his blog, "I Date Outside My Race Because My Race Won't Date Me." In a survey of 396 Asian women from the San Diego area who submitted their profiles to the on-line dating site *match.com*, Hong found that 111 (28%) excluded Asian men from their preferences. Hong, who mostly dates non-Asians, responded, "you're Asian, but you won't date an Asian guy? FUCK YOU! Two can play that game." Not surprisingly, he received a lot of hate mail, for example, "You sound like a bitter Betty. Maybe that's why Asian women won't date you. I wouldn't…not because you're an Asian man, but because you're so short-sighted on humanity." In a subsequent blog, "How I Pissed Off a Bunch of Asian Women on the Internet", an exasperated Hong points out a double standard faced by Asian men. If a black woman criticized black men who admit a preference for white women, she would probably receive wholesale sympathy, not invective.

In their needs and desires, Asian women have more in common with white women than they do with Asian men. They are both initially attracted to tall assertive men. They both seek long-term commitment. Finally, they are both influenced by prevailing stereotypes. I think there are three main reasons why Asian women may prefer white men: assertiveness, status, and an escape from the confines of the Asian family. We have already discussed the first factor. The others are more complex.

The hookers of Pattaya are not in love with their patrons; they love what they can get from them. The intoxication of cash, a glamorous lifestyle, a means of rising above the wretchedness of their birth: these are the things that motivate hundreds of thousands of young Asian women to sell their bodies to lonely strangers from distant shores. For them, the shame of prostitution is less painful than the hopelessness of chronic poverty. Most Asian women earn less in a month than what many white tourists routinely spend on a night out in Bangkok. Just as so many white men are fooled into thinking they are loved by a sweet little Asian girl, so many Asian women fool themselves into thinking they will be saved by a dashing rich white man. Even culture and education offer scant protection from such fanciful thinking. Women everywhere prefer to date men of higher status because it signifies greater potential payoff, and white men, by virtue of their dominant culture, are perceived to have higher status than local men. Asian women often look at Caucasian men not as individuals, but as status symbols. And it is the *perception of status*, rather than actual net worth, which makes the difference. So if an Asian man is as successful or educated or wealthy as his Caucasian counterpart, some Asian women will still find the latter more desirable.

Finally, there is the pressure of living in xenophobically conservative households. Often, Asian parents not only expect their children to marry within their own ethnic fold, but also insist on vetting their partners' every quality. This often leads to an insurmountable conflict between filial obligation and romantic freedom. For many young Asian women, it's liberating to go out with men who neither know about nor care for the stifling prejudices of Asian parents and culture. Rightly or wrongly, they tend to perceive the white men willing to date them as being more open-minded and generous than the Asian men they are not willing to date.

But liberation comes with a price. In her book, *The Asian Mystique,*

123

journalist Sheridan Prasso describes the plight of a young Japanese woman who married a white American. When she first came to the United States as a wide-eyed exchange student, Yukie felt disdain for the authoritarian rigidity and sexism she saw in her parents' marriage. She longed to embrace American egalitarianism and self-determination. A few years later, she met Chris. At first, Yukie was attracted to his self-confident demeanor and reassured by his attentiveness. He told her she was beautiful just being herself, and to forget all the crazy expectations and obligations she may have had at home. But after they had kids, things gradually began to change. Chris became less ambitious, more demanding, less willing to listen to his wife's concerns. It seemed he really wanted a traditional Japanese wife, after all. Yukie changed too. She wanted the children to be raised with knowledge of Japanese traditions, and she wanted to mend the rifts she created with her own parents. But Chris would have none of it. Even after she convinced him to live in Japan, he refused to learn Japanese and resented her parents' intrusions. Eventually they had a bitter divorce. Ironically for Yukie, as Prasso remarks, "in seeking more power in her own marriage that her mother had in hers, she ended up with even less."

Western culture is qualitatively different from East Asian culture in its emphasis on individual autonomy and rights. Over the last century, women living in the West have enjoyed more privileges and upward mobility. But cultures are also fluid, all individuals are unique, and stereotypes do not always reflect reality. As Asian societies modernize their economies, they also tend to liberalize their social values, including women's rights. Many Asian men are indeed boorish louts who enjoy dominating their wives, just like many Caucasian men. But more often than not, Asian couples enjoy mutually respectful and affectionate marriages, perhaps even more so than Westerners. The domineering Asian husband and his submissive kowtowing wife is an exaggeration of a traditional public role that fails to appreciate what really happens in private: Asian women have always had a lot more power and influence behind closed doors than many in the West realize. And marriages everywhere work better when grounded in common values, a shared culture and language, and a network of mutual friends and relatives. Asians tend to be stronger in these departments than Americans. Interracial marriages are often even more lacking in these supports. Like sexual attraction itself, the allure of the opposite can blinding at first, but unbearably light at the end.

The reasons why white men are attractive to Asian women should also apply to the preferences of Asian men. Being from the dominant culture, Caucasian women, especially if young and attractive, can elevate the status of the Asian man able to get them. And, of course, marrying a white woman eliminates the parental expectation and pressure of having to marry an Asian woman. But the difference between Asian male and female interracial mating outcome comes down to the fact that women usually do the choosing. For all the reasons I discussed, especially the Asian man's lack of self-confidence, white women are generally less attracted to Asian men than Asian women are to white men. But it takes two to tango. It's no secret that there are legions of Caucasian men completely obsessed with the notion of Asian femininity.

Yellow Fever

We are now ready to tackle the so-called "Asian fetish". According to Sheridan Prasso, of the thousands of websites devoted to sexual fetishes (S&M, leather and vinyl, feet, large breasts, and so on), those related to Asian women are by far the most common. There are literally hundreds of dating services and escort agencies catering exclusively to Caucasian men with "yellow fever". In stark contrast, there are very few aimed at Asian men interested in "white meat". I have made it clear that Asian women have more reasons to date Caucasian men than white women have to choose Asian men, but the fact is that internet porn sites and escort agencies are created largely by and for men. Women tend to be repulsed by these kinds of sexual outlets. So the Asian women's interest in white men is reciprocated, albeit in a different form.

Sexual fetish is defined as an obsession with a concept, object, body part, or type of person as a target of arousal. It is a type of *essentialism,* where the attraction is to the essence of the Asian feminine ideal as opposed to the reality of any particular person. Men are much more likely to indulge in them, largely because their sexual appetites are more visually driven. The object of the fetish has characteristics that appeal both to innate sexual desire and to acquired cultural taste, and the two play off each other. For example, being an Anglophile, I have an appreciation of British history. I also have a fetish for attractive English women. My attraction deepens my appreciation; my appreciation kindles my attraction. Many fetishists defend themselves saying there's nothing intrinsically wrong with preference; some gentlemen prefer blondes, others brunettes. We all have our preferences, but preference is still prejudice, and prejudice invokes stereotype. The danger comes when we don't allow the object of our affection to grow beyond stereotype and mature into a full-blooded individual with transcendent qualities and desires. In the words of the psychologist Benjamin Tong, "to discover what a person truly is right from the start is virtually impossible; we bring baggage, we bring projections, and the difficulty in relationships is working through that so that the relating is authentic and real, between human beings who may or may not come close to the stereotype."

The Asian fetish offers a revealing view into the psychology of the white man. When Caucasians who date Asians exclusively are asked what they see in Asian women, the usual responses include the following: "they're all so delicate", "they know exactly how to make love to a man", "they're so exotic and mysterious", "they listen and obey". These encapsulate the four motivations behind the Asian fetish. First, men like variety. Anything exotic therefore tends to be erotic. But this can't be the full answer, because yellow fever is more widespread than "jungle fever" (black fetish). The second reason is Asian anatomy. Neoteny suggests youth, which, in turn, suggests fertility and health. Asians, of both sexes, tend to be of slighter build and have more youthful features than Caucasians of the same age. This appeals to white men (both straight and gay). Third, the combination of foreignness and youthfulness naturally tickle the white man's sex buttons. He then justifies his desire for short-term sex by stereotyping the Asian woman as easy and promiscuous.

The last element of the Asian fetish is that of the submissive domestic servant ready and willing to devote herself to her master's every whim. It's a fantasy fueled by colonial-era stereotypes repackaged by Hollywood. The Asian woman is more than just a whore. She's also a virgin, a naïf, and a Madonna, all at the same time. If you're a white man, you can get the two for one special: an Asian woman for a fling, but also ideal for marriage. The playwright David Henry Hwang points out the absurdity of this stereotype in his play *M Butterfly*, a satiric take on Puccini's *Madame Butterfly*. The play is based on the improbable yet true story of a French diplomat who falls in love with a Chinese opera singer, Song Liling, who turns out to be a spy in drag. Remarkably, the diplomat somehow deludes himself for years into thinking Song to be the woman of his dreams. But she/he reminds him:

> "It's one of your favorite fantasies, isn't it? The submissive Oriental woman and the cruel white man...Consider it this way: what would you say if a blonde homecoming queen fell in love with a short Japanese businessman? He treats her cruelly, then goes home for three years, during which time she prays to his picture and turns down marriage from a young Kennedy. Then, when she learns he has remarried, she kills herself. Now, I believe you would consider this girl to be a deranged idiot, correct? But because it's an Oriental who kills herself for a Westerner – ah! – you find it beautiful."

Thanks to a serendipitous convergence of anatomical and cultural factors, the Asian woman is able to satisfy both sides of the Madonna/whore complex. Unfortunately for Asian men, white women don't share this psychology. But it has not escaped my attention that Asian men do tickle the sexual preferences of gay men. There is no evidence that the rate of homosexuality is higher in Asian populations. In fact, it is probably lower given their highly conservative cultures. But there is much anecdotal evidence that Asian men are more sought after amongst gay white and African American men for the same reasons that Asian women are popular amongst heterosexual non-Asian men. I personally have been approached many more times by gay men (black, white, and Hispanic) who apparently found me attractive than by women (white or Asian) whom I found to be attractive.

I want to make a final point about the Jewish-Asian connection. When I was a medical resident, I had a Jewish colleague who told me he would never marry one of his own. In fact he had only ever dated Asians and was going out with a Filipino nurse at the time. He told me Jewish girls are demanding and neurotic, while Asian girls are gentle and considerate. Whatever the validity of his prejudices, the rate of intermarriage between Jews and Asians has increased dramatically in the last several decades, especially amongst the academic and professional classes. There are the high-profile cases: Facebook mogul Mark Zukerberg and pediatrician Priscilla Chan, talk show host Maury Povich and news anchor Connie Chung, Harvard law professors Noah Feldman and Jeannie Suk (now divorced), Yale law professor Jed Rubenfeld and tiger mom Amy Chua, and the list goes on. A glance at the wedding pages in any major newspaper will tell you just how common such pairings are becoming. And they all seem to have one thing in common: the man is a Jew and the woman is Asian. Presumably the qualities that Asian women and Jewish men find attractive in each other are the qualities that Jews and Asians share: love of learning, drive to succeed, and devotion to family. But Jews and Asians of both sexes possess these traits. Aren't Jewish women attracted to smart, hard-working, family-oriented Asian men? Apparently the factors that keep Asian men and white women apart are enough to trump those factors that bring Asian women and Jewish men together.

**

Evolutionary psychology tells us that men compete against one another for sexual access to a limited pool of willing women. Asian women do at least as well as white women in the interracial dating game. Perhaps they should be flattered by all that attention. But they also have every right to complain when white men see them solely through the lens of the Asian fetish. It is worse for Asian men, who are not only stereotyped, but play second fiddle to men of other races. So what then can be done for people like Kevin?

Perhaps we can take a page out of the feminist playbook. In *The Blank Slate*, Steven Pinker points out that there are two types of feminists. *Equity feminists* are traditional liberals who believe that gender inequality is the result not only of a legacy of discrimination but also the result of some innate biological and psychological differences. *Gender feminists* are Marxist-leaning radicals who deny the very existence of innate differences and maintain that gender inequality is simply the inevitable result of male dominated society. Equity feminists want to maximize the woman's freedom of choice in career and lifestyle and allow her to compete against men on equal terms. But unlike gender feminists, they realize that individuals differ in fundamental ways and so are willing to accept that equal opportunity does not necessarily result in the equality of outcome. And that's not always a bad thing. Steven Pinker so eloquently writes, "equality is not the empirical claim that all groups of humans are interchangeable; it is the moral principle that individuals should not be judged or constrained by the average properties of their group...Inequality of *outcome* cannot be used as proof of inequality of *opportunity* unless the groups being compared are identical in all of their psychological traits, which is likely to be true only if we are blank slates."

This is a healthy debate between those who want to maximize opportunity at cost of some equality versus others who want equity at the cost of some coercion. When it comes to gender, I believe we can justifiably take a libertarian approach, accepting the fact that total equality of outcome is unrealistic when individuals are not naturally identical in talent, temperament, or taste. To impose equality where there is none is as unfair as mistreating those who are less fortunate. Much of the difference between men and women is biological, not cultural. But when it comes to race, the differences are largely social constructs. Racial inequality is more likely to be the result of socio-cultural factors rather than biological ones. If we simply let people do what they want but end up with countless angry Asian men like Kevin, more social engineering is needed.

7

The Content of their Character
The Limits of Meritocracy

A meritocracy is a system in which the people who are the luckiest in their health and genetic endowment; luckiest in terms of family support, encouragement, and probably, income; luckiest in their educational and career opportunities; and luckiest in so many other ways difficult to enumerate – these are the folks who reap the largest rewards.

The only way for even a putative meritocracy to hope to pass ethical muster, to be considered fair, is if those who are the luckiest in all of those respects also have the greatest responsibility to work hard, to contribute to the betterment of the world, and to share their luck with others.

Ben Bernanke
June 2, 2013
Princeton University

Princeton

I am writing this chapter in the glass-rimmed mezzanine of the Lewis-Sigler Institute for Integrative Genomics at Princeton University, housed in an ultra-modern building donated by the billionaire financier Carl Icahn,

Class of '57. Around me are a dozen or so undergraduates, concentrating over their laptops and problem sets, cramming for their midterms in biochemistry or differential equations. They are all Asian. Looking out, I see playing fields ringed by neo-gothic college spires. There's a rugby scrum going on. Most of the players appear to be white.

Princeton was my first love. I applied for early decision in the fall of 1986. I was rejected. I should have expected this, coming in with an SAT score of only 1420 (780 math), and a GPA barely in the top tenth of my class. Seven years later, it was my younger brother's turn. He was a salutatorian and National Merit Scholar who notched an impressive 1540 on his SAT (top 99.9 percentile in the nation). He too was rejected. Soon afterwards, we drafted an ugly letter to the dean of admissions, accusing him of anti-Asian bias and threatening to bring legal action against an institution that we held in such high esteem. I packed a baseball bat into the back of my Honda and drove out to the admissions office after midnight with destructive thoughts on my mind.

The rage and indignation have subsided in the intervening quarter century. I was accepted to many other fine institutions including Dartmouth, Cornell, the University of Pennsylvania, and the University of Chicago, ending up with my hands (and head) full at MIT. My brother graduated from Columbia, where he spent an inordinate amount of time on non-sanctioned extracurricular activities. I went on to medical school, and he became an orthodontist. We could have done worse. Thanks to the sacrifice of our parents and the dedication of our guidance counselors, we've had great educations. Let me now make it clear that I don't feel as if my life trajectory was somehow derailed by Princeton's rebuff. While our personal experience typifies the general Asian American experience with higher education, this chapter is not about my own love-hate relationship with the Ivy League. It is about the complex relationship of fairness, merit, and equality of opportunity, and about the ambiguous way that America has treated its citizens of Asian heritage.

Too Good For Their Own Good

A few years ago, Time Magazine published a cover story entitled "Asians: Are they Making the Grade?" It implied that Asian American students were faceless math and science grinds brainwashed by their parents to study to the test, conditioned to succeed not for their own happiness but out of filial obligation. While content of the piece was outwardly complementary, I detected a hint of fearful resentment underneath. In public and many private high schools throughout the country, it is the Asian students who are setting a high curve, challenging everyone else to claim their valedictory seat, National Merit Scholarship, Intel Science Talent Prize, and All State Orchestra slot. Professor Carolyn Chen, director of the Asian American Studies Program at Northwestern University, wrote in her Op-Ed piece for the New York Times ("Asians: Too Smart for Their Own Good?" Dec 20, 2012): "For middle-class and affluent whites, overachieving Asian Americans pose thorny questions about privilege and power, merit and opportunity. Some white parents have reportedly shied away from selective public schools that have become "too Asian," fearing that their children will be outmatched."

Nowhere has this become more of a reality than in New York City's trio of elite public high schools. Admission is determined solely by the score on a multiple-choice exam. As of 2012, 16% of students in the New York City school system were of Asian descent. But the proportion at Brooklyn Technical High School was 59%. Bronx High School of Science was 63% Asian. And at the most selective public high school of all, Stuyvesant, 72% of the student body was Asian, with blacks and Hispanics making up less than 4%. Alarmed by the racial disparity, African American and Latino groups lobbied (unsuccessfully) to have the admission standards amended so as to make it easier for "disadvantaged minority" students to get in. Countering this sentiment, a number of Asian American alumni pointed out that relaxing admission standards would necessarily adulterate the quality of the education. "Stuyvesant isn't for everyone," one of them said. The reaction amongst white parents was understandably mixed: some supported the ideal of academic meritocracy while others defended the virtues of ethnic inclusivity.

The Challenge From the Left: Affirmative Action

Affirmative action in education was initially legislated in the 1960's as a means of correcting centuries of exclusionary practices designed to keep blacks from positions of authority by keeping them illiterate. Affirmative action's modus operandi was the race-based admission quota. While laudable in intent, the end result was to simply counter a long history of discrimination with another program of reverse discrimination. In the latter half of the twentieth century, only a racist minority wanted to keep black people uneducated. The overwhelming majority of all backgrounds supported equal access to opportunity, a sentiment famously articulated by Martin Luther King, Jr. But by the 1990's, affirmative action's double standard was taking a toll: under-qualified blacks and Hispanics granted lower standards of admission than whites and Asians were suffering from higher dropout rates. At the same time, significant numbers of white and Asian candidates with superior credentials were passed up. Around the country, voters decided that affirmative was a major impediment to meritocracy. In 1999, the State of California passed Proposition 209, which declared race-based admission illegal.

The results were dramatic. By 2006, the proportion of African American freshman at UC Berkeley fell by fifty percent. The same thing happened at the other UC campuses. The ethnic and racial makeup of California is 44% white, 35% Hispanic, 12% Asian, and 7% black, but at Berkeley, the student population is now 46% Asian, 29% white, 11% Hispanic, and only 4% black. Critics of affirmative action point out, however, that the graduation rates of blacks and Latinos have increased significantly in the last decade, presumably because those who were able to enroll were better qualified to begin with. Moreover, the black enrolment in both undergraduate and professional programs has started to recover, although not to pre-209 levels.

The notion that racial preferences lead to a "mismatch" between the natural aptitude of students favored by affirmative action and the academic challenges they face in the schools that accept them has been brought up by academics like UCLA law professor Richard Sander. He found that black students who enrolled in their second choice law school had lower dropout rates than those who attended their presumably more demanding first choice. Supreme Court Justice Clarence Thomas, who admits to having benefitted from affirmative action himself, has stated that many African Americans are hurt by being admitted to schools where they are surrounded by more capable peers. He argues it is better to get rid of affirmative action, which he considers to be another form of discrimination, and focus on a more fundamental problem: fixing the mess in primary public education.

A possible consequence of mismatch is that many otherwise motivated black and Hispanic students tend to steer clear or drop out of STEM (science, technology, engineering, and mathematics) majors. These subjects often require an intimidating set of prerequisites, which beginning students are already expected to have completed before entering college. Students who are shaky on algebra cannot expect to keep up with basic calculus, let alone differential equations. Discouraged from science, many minority students at top universities switch to easier humanities majors. This might not have been the case had they enrolled in less selective institutions from the start.

Affirmative action's damaging impact isn't just limited to those who drop out. Students who remain suffer the effects of negative perception. I remember a painful incident from my freshman chemistry class at MIT. We had a lousy teaching assistant who happened to be African American. Not familiar with the concept of affirmative action, I asked a fellow Korean American student how someone like him could have gotten into the graduate department. He cynically replied, "affirmative action." A few years later, one of my (white) medical school classmates had just failed his anatomy exam. He vented his anger at the black students who had passed because of what he thought was unfair coaching. "They don't deserve to be here!" he yelled in earshot of the minority recruitment office. As laudable a goal as it may be to promote educational opportunities for disadvantaged minorities, affirmative action comes with a psychological cost. Many beneficiaries experience humiliation and self-doubt that can reduce their later achievement.

One institute that proudly eschews all forms of affirmative action or any other form of favoritism, such as alumni perks or athletic scholarships, is the California Institute of Technology. Among the most selective of all colleges, Caltech boasts a median SAT score of over 1500. It is also among the least diverse in terms of disadvantaged minorities. Its student body is 33% Asian and 70% male. Seven percent of the students are Hispanic and less than one percent is black. In fact, of the 207 members of the freshman class of 2004, there was just one African American. Like Stuyvesant, Caltech isn't for everyone. Admission here is determined almost entirely by academics, both in terms of prior achievement, and importantly, in terms of future potential. Special consideration is given to bright high school students from poor backgrounds who have excelled despite the odds. The admission department actually raises the bar for children of faculty or privilege in the belief that they should be held to an even higher standard. As befitting a true meritocracy, Caltech doesn't care about sex or race or class or sports, only about excellence and passion in the pursuit of science.

The Challenge From the Right: Legacy Advantage

In a meritocracy, excellence effervesces to the surface. But not everyone can be excellent. Most of us are mired in the morass of mediocrity below. It's a curious fact that the ruling classes of nations are seldom the excellent classes. One reason for this is the concept of *regression to the mean*: an unusual occurrence is likely to be followed by a more typical one. Both natural ability and social influence are distributed on a bell curve. Excellence is rare, but mediocrity is common. But social influence is easy to pass on through culture or money, while natural ability is largely genetic and unpredictable. So power tends to be inherited by the weaker descendants of strong rulers rather than the other way around. Weak kings ride the inertia of their stronger forebears. Over generations, power ossifies, while natural ability regresses to the mean. A second reason is the concept of *loss aversion*: those with something to lose will fight harder to keep it than others will fight to gain it. This makes it easier for rulers to maintain control than for the ruled to depose them. Loss aversion applies to politics, wealth, fame, and war. Unlike the Old World, where history matters, the United States has never really had a hereditary aristocracy or landed gentry. New money is as good as old: it matters less where it came from than how much you have. But those who have it also tend to be better at making more of it, relative to everyone else. In this country, the perpetuation of wealth and privilege doesn't come from title or land but from connections. The best way to become rich and powerful is to have rich and powerful friends. And it helps to develop these friendships early in life.

Education may be the road to success, but it's better paved for some than for others. This is especially true when it comes to the relationship between the upper classes and the elite universities. The stranglehold that wealthy families have endeavored to maintain on their children's access to higher education at the cost of those less well off is the second major challenge to meritocracy. Unlike affirmative action, which at least has some moral credibility, the advantages of legacy and wealth are purely opportunistic. Yet this is precisely why this enemy from the right is unlikely to be defeated anytime soon.

Over the last half-century, community colleges and public universities have done a pretty good job of educating disadvantaged minorities and the poor. Through state funding and affirmative action, African Americans have attained higher rates of literacy and vocational competency than ever before. Average family income has increased. Most households own cars and fancy televisions. Everyone has Internet. No one is starving. Politically, America seems to be more inclusive and democratic. But the gloss of progressivism masks a disturbing underlying inequality. Top CEO's now earn 300 times more than their average employee, yet their tax rates are hardly any higher. The top one percent of households owns more than half of all wealth but pays less than a fifth of all taxes. A net worth of a billion dollars is not enough to get you into the Forbes 400 list. The right tail of the wealth curve is indeed very long and growing. If any wealth ever trickles down, it's microscopic. The net result is that the children of the rich are more likely to stay rich while the children of the poor are more likely to remain impoverished than they were a generation ago. Thanks to unregulated stock markets, regressive tax codes, and plain corporate greed, the United States is now the most socially immobile nation in the industrialized world.

A major source of economic inequality comes from the marriage of convenience between the elite classes and the elite universities. For generations, the wealthy have incubated their networks of legalized kleptocracy in the secret societies and eating clubs of Princeton and Yale. The rich inoculate themselves from the democratic influence of the hoi polloi by barricading themselves behind the ivy-festooned gates of the college quad. They have the influence to get themselves in and the money to keep others out. But increasingly, their privileged position has come under threat from immigrant Asian upstarts.

We've seen this movie before. In the early decades of the last century, the Yankee domination of the Ivy League was challenged by the children of Eastern European immigrants. Fiercely ambitious and inured to the hardships of their parents, these children readily mastered not only English, but also the Latin, Greek, and other archaic subjects needed to get into the top schools. They had surpassed the WASPs at their own game. Between 1900 and 1922, the Jewish enrolment at Harvard increased from seven to twenty-two percent. By 1918, Columbia University was over forty percent Jewish. Alarmed at the prospect of their children being outcompeted by the massive influx of more talented foreigners, the WASP establishment came up with a crafty set of measures to stem the tide.

The first was alumni preference. Since most alumni already belonged to the establishment, guaranteed admission for their children would effectively propagate their domination into the next generation. The fact that many of them also served on their alma mater's board of directors was a convenient conflict of interest. This racket was rather similar to the exclusionary immigration laws put into effect in the 1920's that set quotas on the ethnicities of new arrivals scaled to the proportion of each group already living in the country. Since whites greatly outnumbered Asian citizens to begin with, these measures actually reduced the Asian share of the population until the passage of the Immigration Reform Act of 1965. Legacy preference accomplished the same job in the university setting. By 1936, the proportion of Yale freshmen with an alumnus parent or grandparent approached thirty percent. Meanwhile, the proportion of Jewish undergraduates fell by a third between 1927 and 1934, a period in which the Jewish population actually increased significantly.

Another instrument of discrimination was student athletics. While most of us equate the term with the preponderance of African Americans dominating Division I basketball and football, most student athletes were originally whites recruited from private schools. The sports that got them in were, and still are, largely unfashionable with and inaccessible to working class children living in large cities. They include squash, sailing, crew, water polo, fencing, and horseback riding. While these "snob sports" have now become more mainstream, the students who are proficient enough in them to gain special admission to the elite universities are still predominantly upper class whites. For example, varsity skiers and lacrosse players are more than 90% white. More recently, the push for women's athletics in the wake of the Title IX gender equality law has had a dramatic impact on college admissions, but perhaps not the one originally intended by its liberal-minded legislators. Instead of achieving the laudable goal of sexual parity, which is no longer necessary given that more than half of all college students are now women, it merely lowered the bar for the daughters of the white upper class at the cost of disadvantaged minorities. College recruiters are encouraged to pursue these demographics because athletic success equates to massive infusions of revenue from their parents.

This brings us to the third preference: the rich and famous. Private universities always want more money, sometimes at the cost of compromising their core mission of fair education. In a self-propagating cycle, money is required to attract top professors and to build state of the art research facilities, which are necessary to spark award-winning discoveries and breakthroughs, which in turn enhance the prestige of the university and bring in more money, much of it from wealthy donors who like to pride themselves as refined patrons of the arts and sciences. But these donors often want something else in return. Some shamelessly offer their gift on the condition that the school accepts their child. Fortunately for them, the admissions departments and the fund-rasing departments of many elite universities are incestuously intertwined. Applications from the children of wealthy donors, many of which wouldn't make the cut the usual way, are assigned to a separate pool. So it's a simple fact that the larger the donation a parent makes, the more likely his child will be offered admission as a way of giving thanks. Since the upper classes are more likely to make big donations to the top schools, their children are more likely to become students there. In many cases, the donors also happen to be alumni, in which case admission is virtually assured.

When I was a graduate student at Oxford in the fall of 1990, I met a cocky bleached-blond kid just out of a prep school in California who hardly ever studied for his introductory Shakespeare tutorial and seemed to spend most of his time smoking pot with a small group of rich Americans. With envious curiosity, I asked him what he was doing. He told me he was taking a year off to experience Europe, ski the Alps, sail the Caribbean, and go on safari in Kenya before enrolling at Harvard the following year. It was only many years later that I realized he was probably on their semi-secret "Z-list". These are academically borderline cases (about 25 to 50 each year) that would have no chance of getting into Harvard the usual way. But because their parents are big donors, the admissions board obsequiously grants them deferred admissions. The university is happy to get a big check. The parents are happy their kid wasn't rejected. And the kid is happy to spend his gap year jet setting around the world. Everyone wins.

The most prominent names bring so much positive publicity that universities actively court their children even if they are neither alumni nor donors. Most expected John F. Kennedy Jr. to attend Harvard, like his father and grandfather before him. But Brown University's admissions director James Rogers, aware of his distaste for math and his poor academic record in private school, campaigned hard to convince him and his mother of the virtues of Brown's open-ended undergraduate curriculum. It worked. Rogers later admitted, "the greatest advantage to Brown I was able to achieve was the admission and matriculation of John. People began to talk about Brown." After he graduated in 1983 with a degree in drama, Kennedy went on to flunk his bar exam twice.

The New Jews

In 2006, Yale freshman Jian Li filed a complaint with the Department of Education's Office of Civil Rights alleging that Princeton University denied him admission based on his Asian background (he was also rejected by Harvard, Stanford, MIT and the University of Pennsylvania). Li, who had a perfect score on the SAT and was ranked in the top one percent of his high school class, didn't receive much sympathy; after all, he got into Yale. Many felt he was making a mountain out of a molehill. The Ivies often reject top students of all races, and Asians are already overrepresented at the elite schools. But Li was making a bigger point: Asian Americans are unfairly held to a higher standard at places like Princeton.

Asian students consistently score higher on their SAT's, take more AP classes, and attain higher GPA's and class ranks than other races. In 2006, 32% of National Merit Scholars, 27% of Presidential Scholars, and 40% of Intel Science Talent Search finalists were of Asian descent, yet their proportion at the Ivy League was only 15%. A study funded by the Center for Equal Opportunity in Virginia found that the average SAT score for Asians admitted to the University of Michigan in 2005 was

1400 (out of 1600), while the average for whites was 1350, the average for Hispanics was 1260, and the average for blacks was only 1160. In other words, Asians had to make up a 240-point deficit compared with blacks. Top universities claim to reward academic excellence, but the numbers don't seem to add up.

There's no question that affirmative action deserves much blame. But that's only part of the problem. In their book, *No Longer Separate, Not Yet Equal*, Princeton sociologists Thomas Espenshade and Alexandria Radford did extensive modeling of admissions data for all 245,000 applicants to eight highly selective public and private academic institutions in 1983, 1993, and 1997. They found that if affirmative action were eliminated for the freshman class of 1997, the proportion of accepted black students would fall by 57%. The positive effects on Asians and whites would be a modest 9% gain in both cases. However, if *all* preferences other than academic merit were discounted, including legacy advantages, donor preferences, celebrity cases, athletic scholarships, and the like, the results would be quite different. Here, the negative impact would be felt by both white applicants, whose acceptance rate would fall by 11%, as well as by black and Hispanic applicants (66% and 40% losses respectively). On the other hand, Asian acceptances would soar 63%. Under a completely meritocratic policy, the top universities would be expected to be 53% white, 5% Hispanic, 3% black, and 39% Asian. This would bring the Asian share more in line with their high school academic performance. Daniel Golden, author of the revealing expose, *The Price of Admission: How America's Ruling Class Buys Its Way into Elite Colleges—and Who Gets Left Outside the Gates* writes, "overall, Asian Americans are the odd group out, lacking racial preferences enjoyed by other minorities and the advantages of wealth and lineage mostly accrued by upper-class whites. This second-class status stymies Asian aspirations to join the country's inner circle of political, economic, and social leaders; limits that leadership circle's exposure to bright minds with fresh ideas; and breeds cynicism among Asian students and parents who emigrated here in search of opportunity..."

It would seem that Asian Americans get shafted from both ends of the political spectrum. But the picture is more than just black and white. A common complaint amongst both high school guidance counselors and college admission officers is that all those Kims and Lees start to look alike.

This is not necessarily a racist stereotype. Golden quotes one of them as saying almost in exasperation, "you get a group of them. Every single child has had music lessons. Every single child succeeds well in math. Every single child has done community service in a hospital. Every child has done Chinese or Korean studies on Saturdays and is fluent in that language. You're writing the same letter again and again." This is a loaded message. There's nothing inherently wrong with Asians making up 40% or even 70% of our top universities if they so qualify. The hidden question seems to be: do we really want our best universities filled with one-dimensional math and science grinds? The perception that Asian American students tend to be generic cookie-cutter pre-med types is unfortunate, but not entirely inaccurate. Students should have the freedom to study whatever they choose. But universities also have the prerogative to teach whatever they want. There are places to learn medicine and science. There are also places for the liberal arts. No university should be expected to cater to "texture-less math grinds" regardless of ethnic origin. The fact that Asian children are so often molded by their parents and culture to quietly follow well-worn paths that worked for their ancestors has hurt them in a society that values innovation and extroversion. Until Asians learn to expand their repertoire, they'll continue to be screwed at the admissions department.

The Jews mastered these harsh lessons early on. Faced with blatant anti-Semitism from the WASP establishment a century ago, they founded their own medical and law schools, generously endowed them with millions of dollars, and nurtured their children to excel in all fields of knowledge. Through their institutions, inventions, and discoveries, greatly aided by the influx of intellectuals fleeing Nazi Europe, the Jews transformed America from a cultural backwater to an artistic and scientific powerhouse second to none. And once the establishment realized the value of Jewish talent, it was no longer fashionable to discriminate against them. Today, many universities go out of their way to build Hillel centers and sponsor recruitment drives in the Jewish enclaves of Beverly Hills and Long Island. Jewish kids have cracked the admissions code, allowing them to achieve dominance in business, law, medicine, the arts, the natural and social sciences, and the media. And most importantly, they can now pass on the benefits of legacy and wealth to their own children. In transforming

America, the Jews have also transformed themselves into an integral part of the power structure.

The perception of the Asian student as a nameless faceless robot is partly self-inflicted, but it's also partly the result of implicit biases. In chapter two, I discussed how racial stereotypes are a natural outcome of the instinctive human tendency to generalize the unfamiliar. White admissions officers with limited exposure to Asian culture or Asians in general will tend to generalize them into bite-size stereotypes: Yoon does well in math, practices violin, wants to be a doctor, and speaks Korean at home, just like all the others. Especially given the monolithic face they so often show to outsiders, Asian kids are understandably perceived as generic categories and not as the complex individuals they usually are. White applicants aren't perceived this way. The fact that the folks in admissions have racially biased perceptions doesn't imply that they're bad people. In a sense, we are all born racists. The problem is when they make important decisions based on those subconscious perceptions.

Over the last few decades, social psychologists have used the implicit association test (IAT) as a way to measure how subconscious biases affect conscious judgment. The results are surprising. It's not just self-confessed bigots who have negative attitudes towards other races. Many who consider themselves open-minded liberals nonetheless harbor significant negative subconscious racism. For example, when shown images of the actors Kate Winslet and Lucy Liu, followed by a brief (subconsciously perceived) flash of the words "foreign" and "American", most people associated Liu with foreign, even when they knew that Winslet is British and Liu is American. The power of implicit association in influencing conscious decision-making should not be underestimated.

The generalization of Asians as a singular identity based on shared physiognomy is largely valid. But it becomes much less so when based on shared cultural characteristics and academic habits. It's wrong to treat all individuals within a group based on characteristics common to many members of that group. Asians are not monolithic. Korean and Filipino cultures have about as much in common as Russian and Italian cultures. Many Scots are insulted when confused with the English. Koreans are even more insulted when mistaken for Japanese. And within each of these groupings there is tremendous variability. Indonesians are as diverse as Americans, for example. But once implicit racism takes hold, people are much less willing to see these distinctions. What may be a fair assessment of some people of a given race is not a fair assessment of every person of that race. And de-individualization can be the first step towards de-humanization, a progression down a slippery slope that has been used time and again to justify discrimination, hostility, and worse. Slavery, apartheid, and the Holocaust are prime examples. Asian Americans face nothing that severe. But injustice exists. Illiterate Laotian and Cambodian refugees fleeing from war and genocide are very different from sweatshop Chinese immigrants from Guangdong Province, who are altogether different again from South Koreans on student visas. If affirmative action and alumni preferences have hurt the children of East Asian immigrants, they have devastated those of impoverished Southeast Asians, who truly are disadvantaged minorities. When it comes to college applications, the "Asian American" category is worse than useless. It's downright deleterious.

The Limits of Meritocracy

Meritocracy is a concept deeply rooted in both the political tradition of utilitarianism, first articulated by Jeremy Bentham, and in the economic tradition of market capitalism, as described by Adam Smith in *Wealth of Nations*. These two giants of eighteenth century British moral philosophy applied Enlightenment rationalism to normative ethics, the study of how people ought to behave towards one another in an ideal world. Bentham quite reasonably believed that humans are driven primarily by the pursuit of pleasure and the avoidance of pain. In his philosophy, right and wrong is reduced to a simple hedonic calculus. The ideal state is one in which the greatest happiness is enjoyed by the greatest number of its citizens. He argued that this goal is most likely to be attained through a minimalist government that at once protects its citizens from tyranny and nurtures productivity through private ownership free of onerous taxation. From this marriage of utilitarianism and the free market came the modern concept of libertarianism.

Libertarians acknowledge the existence and differential distributions of the four T's: talent, temperament, taste, and treasure. Treasure is the measure of actual wealth, net worth, or, in the case of nation states, GNP, at a given point in time. It is derived from potential wealth, which is a function of the other three T's. Talent can refer to intelligence, physical prowess, or other raw ability. Temperament refers to one's motivation and drive for success. Taste pertains to the quality and quantity of one's happiness elicited by a particular situation or event. Talent, temperament, and taste are largely inherited traits that vary from person to person. Therefore, their distributions are Gaussian (bell-shaped) curves. But treasure tends to be much more skewed to the right, where most wealth is concentrated. Let me give you an analogy. Imagine wealth distributed on a graphic equalizer whose setting can be changed by a dimmer switch. Libertarians believe that this dimmer switch should be set very loose. The invisible hand of the free market and a minimalist caretaker government will ensure that treasure is a thin liquid that flows throughout the population based solely on talent, temperament, and taste. This is, in fact, what happens in a pure meritocracy. People are allowed to work to their potential, but because some are more or less productive than others, and some are more or less motivated than others, not everyone will end up with the same outcome. Moreover because some enjoy the fruits of their labor more or less then others, one should not assume that the poor are less happy than the wealthy. In a utilitarian world, people deserve what they get.

There is much to be said for libertarianism. First of all, it makes a lot of sense. Human beings have a unique capacity for reason thanks to their oversized prefrontal cortex, which enables conscious decision-making. In Bentham's ideal world, a sea of rational free agents making informed decisions would necessarily optimize utility. Unfortunately, he made two fatal assumptions. The first was that if left alone, people consciously and rationally decide to maximize their own happiness. We are homo economicus. The second was that if the actions of free individuals are summed up over the entire population, the aggregate well being of the group is likewise maximized. Let's examine each in turn.

People make irrational decisions all the time. In fact, most choices are made subconsciously. If the mind is an iceberg, consciousness is just the brilliant chunk jutting up above the surface. The massive subconscious darkness lurking beneath is impulsive, selfish, and prone to self-deception. Moreover, it's been designed by natural selection to favor behaviors that are more likely to get its owner's genes into the next generation than to make him any happier. These include the endless pursuit of fame, fortune, and females. But time and again, studies have found that insatiable lust and greed only leads to anxiety and depression. As the psychologist Arthur C. Brooks, paraphrasing the Buddha, puts it, "it's better to want what you have than to have what you want…love people and use things", not the other way around.

If people can't be trusted to maximize their own happiness, how can societies based on libertarian freedom possibly be expected to maximize theirs? Unregulated free markets concentrate power and wealth at the top where it tends to expand and congeal simply because those at the top have the means and the motivation to hold on to it and make more of it. But this is no recipe for happiness because of the marginal return of wealth on happiness: the more you have, the more you need to make you happier. Meanwhile, the masses on the bottom (where there is more correlation between wealth and happiness) have neither. Laissez-faire economics a la Adam Smith will not maximize utility the way Bentham imagined. It is clear that libertarianism, and its mantra of meritocracy, has natural limits.

The Fairness of Equality

Jeremy Bentham may have suffered from Asperger syndrome. He never married, and was described by his peers as socially inept and oddly pedantic in his mannerisms. His approach to life was rigidly ritualized. He was a mentalizer, not an empathizer. And it was this lack of empathy that undermined his moral philosophy. In chapter four, I described Jonathan Haidt's moral foundations theory. In this view of human nature, the mind is compartmentalized into six moral spheres: empathy, liberty, fairness, loyalty, authority, and sanctity. Liberals emphasize the first three and ignore the rest. Libertarians focus almost exclusively on liberty and fairness. Conservatives hold all six moral foundations in equal regard. The value of freedom and the fairness of reciprocal altruism are obvious to the rational mind. But empathy requires something extra. What libertarians fail to realize is that fairness has as much to do with empathy and community as it does with freedom.

Empathy has evolutionary roots in the oxytocin-secreting synapses and mirror neurons that enabled mothers to bond with their babies and lovers to bond with each other wordlessly. It involves neural circuits that control facial expression and gaze detection. Eventually, empathy also enabled communication and socialization among family, friends, neighbors, and even strangers in the elevator. Evolution selected the genes that create the neural basis of empathy because it's a quick and easy way of expressing one's internal states to others without having to resort to language. Expressions are worth a thousand words. But there was another surprising spin-off. Just as your emotions link your mind to the physical state of your body and vice versa (embodied cognition), empathy links you to other minds in other bodies. It makes you want to do unto strangers as you would have them do unto you. Whether or not this makes evolutionary sense, it set in motion the foundations of trust and charity, the cornerstones of liberalism.

The task of uncovering libertarian utilitarianism's most serious flaws was left to Bentham's great disciple, John Stuart Mill. The first flaw was the notion that the end justifies the means, and the second was that people should be treated equally despite differences in their innate talents, temperaments, and tastes. He addressed the need to protect the happiness of minorities from the tyranny of the majority. He also articulated the distinctions between refined and base pleasures and the people who choose to pursue one over the other. Mill's progressive brand of utilitarianism, as propounded in his treatise, *On Liberty*, makes it clear that "mankind are greater gainers by suffering each other to live as seems good to themselves than by compelling each to live as seems good to the rest." Modern libertarianism and liberalism take off from the divide between Bentham and Smith's free market and its emphasis on proportional fairness on the one hand and Mill's empathy-based progressivism on the other.

Libertarians are more individualistic than liberals (and much more so than conservatives). There may be some genetic and neurological basis for this. For example, those who espouse libertarian ideals may also have relatively sluggish dopamine receptors in their brains, which make them easily bored by routine and thus more prone to seek novelty (and also more susceptible to attention deficit disorder). How ironic then that it is the liberals who put more value on the individual than libertarians do. This is because liberals are more sensitive to the pain and suffering of the poor and the sick. They are more likely to see injustice in the oppression and exploitation of others. Where libertarians accept inequality, liberals feel the need to correct it.

Libertarians may be good at understanding their own happiness, but they are bad at understanding the happiness of others. So how can selfish libertarians bent on maximizing their own happiness possibly maximize the aggregate welfare of the group? Liberals believe that we need a leftward bias on the graphic equalizer to redistribute (and therefore maximize) happiness. They call for affirmative action.

The liberal idea of social engineering is to set the dimmer switch to a leftward bias, so there is smooth mobility up the socio-economic ladder, but more resistance with increasing wealth. This requires redistributive taxation of the rich to provide a welfare safety net for the less fortunate. The optimal slope of the tax curve (which determines the size of the net) will depend on how much inequality one wants to eliminate. There is a trade off: too much redistribution will stifle ambition at the top and diminish aggregate treasure; too little concentrates it with a tiny minority. Finding the right balance has been the challenge for modern capitalist democracies.

Liberals and libertarians alike champion equality of opportunity because they agree that hard work, talent, and good taste should be rewarded. But liberals also call for some equality of outcome because those at the bottom will never be rewarded otherwise. It is more natural to be compassionate towards the less fortunate, the less talented, and the less successful, than it is to deny them charity on meritocratic principles. We are not homo economicus. Our moral compasses are not set to the magnetic attraction of reason alone. It's much easier to support affirmative action when framed this way. But this doesn't mean that affirmative action should get a free pass.

In order to pass ethical muster, affirmative action must prove two things. First, it must demonstrate that those receiving it truly are disadvantaged, and second, it must prove that correcting the disadvantage increases aggregate welfare. Let's examine point one. There is no doubt that African Americans, Hispanics, Native Americans, and many Asian Americans were terribly brutalized and/or marginalized by the white man in recent centuries. Or that many white people did the same to one another for even longer. Many of their descendants are still languishing in poverty and underemployment largely as a result of historical mistreatment. But the proximate reason for their destitution is precisely that: they are poor. This matters far more than ultimate causes like their racial background, or the fact that their ancestors may have been enslaved or evicted from their homelands. Addressing past injustices may be symbolically (and legally) important, but is less so than challenging existing inequality. The factor common to all disadvantaged minorities is economic hardship. It therefore makes much more sense to grant affirmative action based on financial need than on race. A child of impoverished Hmong refugees who scores slightly below the cutoff for admission to Princeton should benefit more than a child of upper class African American professionals with the same score.

The only rationale for race-based affirmative action is if one can prove that the average aptitude of the group in question, corrected for confounders like poverty, crime, poor schools, etc., is inherently inferior. This sounds unacceptably racist, but if true, it would be the most just course of action. Studies have found that African Americans, as a demographic, are disadvantaged to the extent that replacing traditional race-based affirmative action with one based on economic need (which would level the playing field for poor whites and Asians with those in the upper classes) would still leave them significantly underrepresented at top tier universities. If this inequality cannot be corrected any other way, a modest racial quota would be justifiable on compassionate grounds.

The second point concerns the question of benefit. What is the utility of admitting less qualified applicants to university if they're unlikely to succeed? They're likely to incur the animosity of the more qualified individuals they've displaced and perhaps end up plagued by self-doubt as well. Liberals often say that diversity is a laudable goal in its own right. But is it really? Surveys have found that people living in ethnically mixed neighborhoods in large cities tend to self-segregate. They do this not because they're racist or fearful but because they simply feel more comfortable being around folks they're familiar with. If given a choice, most people naturally gravitate towards others with whom they share a common language, customs, beliefs, interests, and prejudices. This is true even for those who consider themselves "liberal". The empathy module simply works better when it has more to work with. When people are forced to associate with total strangers, sometimes things work out well, but usually only when they discover mutual commonalities. Racial integration may indeed be a laudable goal on paper, but not when it's foisted on people. Everyone should have the freedom to associate with whomever they want. But diversity alone doesn't create cohesion, it creates anomie. This is readily apparent if you visit any university student center or campus cafeteria. There are mixed race tables to be sure, but there are many more self-segregated ones.

Affirmative Action for the Asian Sportsman

We can apply this logic to the tendentious issue of competitive sports and the Asian man. After watching the Chinese American basketball player Jeremy Lin's electrifying performance against Kobe Bryant and the Los Angeles Lakers in February 2012, I have to admit I felt a rousing sense of pride that I hadn't experienced since tennis pro Michael Chang's equally unreal triumph at the French Open a quarter century before. But like Chang before him, Lin's shooting star proved transient. He soon settled into a role as a modest second-string player. The overachieving Chang eventually reached a career high ranking of number two in the world in 1996, but was never again able to win another major. When Kei Nishikori made it to the finals of the US Open in 2014, it was the first time since Michael Chang that an ethnic Asian male made it past the quarterfinals of any grand slam tennis tournament. It's no secret that Asian men are woefully underrepresented in any professional sport that really matters. The number of world-famous Asian sports stars can be counted on one hand. There are two interrelated reasons for this. As you may have guessed, the first is biological and the second is cultural.

As I explained in chapter three in the context of intelligence, the average biological differences among the races are slight. But at the extreme far end of the distribution curve, some of those differences become significant. For example, West Africans, which include the ancestors of most African Americans and Caribbean blacks, have a higher density of fast-twitch muscle fibers packed into their legs. This enables them to sprint a bit faster and jump a bit higher on average than people of other races. This otherwise unremarkable distinction becomes very apparent at the top levels of track and field and basketball. It explains the remarkable fact that every medal awarded in the sprint events at the 2012 Summer Olympics went to runners of West African descent. On the other hand, East Africans, including Kenyans and Ethiopians, have a higher density of slow twitch muscle fibers, which enables them to perform slightly better in long distance running. Not surprisingly, 80% of all international marathon champions of the last decade were of East African descent. The fact that black athletes dominate professional basketball, football, and track is a result of small genetic differences magnified by intense selective competition and the peculiar demands of sports they play.

East Asians are generally of slighter build and height than most Caucasians and Africans (although some African groups, such as the pygmies of the Kalahari, are among the smallest of all humans). As a result, athletes of East Asian descent are at a distinct disadvantage in sports that involve strength and size when compared with both blacks and whites. These include some of the most popular international sports, including tennis and basketball. This is in addition to the disadvantage they share with whites in sprints and marathons when compared with blacks as mentioned previously. The genetics and physiology of race matter at the top levels of professional sports. But from a practical standpoint, athletic advantage has little intrinsic value because it's just an arbitrary product of cultural selection. Sport offers no benefit for natural selection (although its benefit for sexual selection is a totally different matter). Basketball was invented by a Canadian physical education instructor in 1891. Rugby, association football (soccer), and modern tennis were all developed in Victorian England. The reason that white Europeans and Americans initially dominated these sports was largely historical. The reason why blacks and Caucasians dominate them now is largely biological. If East Asians had developed these sports to better fit their physiques, the results would be quite different. Table tennis, gymnastics, speed skating, and martial arts are examples of sports that require agility, flexibility, speed, and balance. Asians suffer no disadvantages there.

Do Asians deserve affirmative action in sports? There is little doubt that Asian men face a natural disadvantage in sports developed by Europeans and better suited to a larger male physique. The reverse may be said for white men and gymnastics. But the difference is that global popular culture is bathed in an intense European-American field potential. So long as tennis is more popular than ping pong, and basketball is more widely watched than sepaktakraw (a lightning-fast Southeast Asian game that resembles a combination of soccer and volleyball), the world famous Asian sportsman will remain a rare commodity indeed. But what would be the value of giving Asian basketball and tennis players a handicap advantage? Wouldn't that have cheapened Michael Chang's legendary victory over Ivan Lendl or Jeremy Lin's tremendous game against the Lakers? Wouldn't Lendl fans and Lakers' fans have cried foul? Chang and Lin certainly wouldn't have taken the offer. Victory is sweeter when the odds are greater. But more victories are better than none. I'll bet that some fans would be willing to pay a small price against meritocracy to see a fellow Asian man succeed a little more often. I know I would. Equal opportunity is better than unearned equality. But opportunity gained by tweaking a gamed system is preferable to a system that offers no opportunity at all. Giving handicap advantage to underrepresented Asian sportsmen is as fair (or unfair) as granting affirmative action to underrepresented African American college applicants. There is no easy solution to the problem of pseudo-meritocracy.

Inclusive Conservatism

There are two really wondrous things about the brain. The first is its tendency to create conscious models of itself. The other is its ability to forge virtual communities of like-minded individuals. Neuroscientists and laymen alike tend to focus on consciousness, but community is perhaps even more consequential. In the course of evolution, organisms that were able to cooperate in groups often had a survival advantage over those who remained single. The most extreme examples of this were the rise of eukaryotes from cooperative bacteria and the emergence of multicellularity. This eventually led to the selection of genes that built neural circuits that enabled groupish behavior. Group selection is still a controversial topic amongst evolutionary biologists who are convinced that the gene is the ultimate level of selection. But there's no doubt that selfish genes can build cooperative organisms. When circumstances make cooperation more advantageous, cooperative individuals are more likely to pass on their genes along with all the behaviors and cognitive glitches that made them more cooperative in the first place.

Buddhist monks teach that suffering comes from our own selfishness. Only by breaking the cycle of recurrent desire can we reach Nirvana. Hindu mystics remind us that our petty consciousnesses prevent us from realizing our oneness with the cosmos. Christian saints believed that charity was the path to salvation. Liberation comes from the annihilation of the self. The psychologist Mihaly Csikszentmihalyi has found that true happiness comes from losing ourselves in a task that's both challenging and engrossing. Happiness also comes from cheering in unison at a soccer match, taking ecstasy, dancing at raves, and engaging in other rhythmic, repetitive behaviors, especially in the presence of others. They all release dopamine, the brain's reward juice, while shutting down the prefrontal regions of the brain that produce self-consciousness. People who belong to sports leagues, social organizations, and churches tend to report higher levels of well-being than those who don't, regardless of income, age, and general health. Happiness does seem to come from selflessness. The conservative New York Times columnist David Brooks writes: "most people don't form a self and then lead a life. They are called by a problem, and the self is constructed gradually by their calling...fulfillment is a byproduct of how people engage their tasks, and can't be pursued directly. Most of us are egotistical and most are self-concerned most of the time, but it's nonetheless true that life comes to a point only in those moments when the self dissolves into some task. The purpose in life is not to find yourself. It's to lose yourself."

When it comes to happiness, indulging our selfish desires is clearly not a long-term solution because our innate nature has a distinct groupish overlay. In the words of Jonathan Haidt, humans are "ninety percent chimp and ten percent bee". There are two important caveats here. First, self-consciousness cannot be turned off completely, no matter how enmeshed one becomes within the group. Individuality can't be totally annihilated, which is precisely why the human condition is such a struggle. The ideal commonwealth is a state that best serves the needs of its individual constituents, rather than an end in and of itself. The second point is that groups are inherently selfish. Humans create in-groups to compete against out-groups, not to love all mankind unconditionally. The persistence of individualism and the selfishness of groups mean that there will always be losers and winners. Groupishness evolved to shift selfishness from the individual to the collective. It cannot eliminate desire or competition. This is why idealistic ideologies like Marxism are doomed to fail and why John Lennon's brotherhood of man, as beautiful as it sounds, are just idealistic words of a dreamer.

Groupishness has a normal distribution. Some people are born with genes that make them more prone to dopamine rushes while socializing or praying. Others are not. This evolved human characteristic is expressed through the moral spheres of loyalty, authority, and sanctity. Those who feel more connected to family and country, have more respect for bosses and law enforcement, and believe in preachers and scriptures are more likely to be drawn to groups than are libertarians and liberals. Once within those groups, they accumulate what Haidt calls "moral capital". In his words: "moral systems are interlocking sets of values, virtues, norms, practices, identities, institutions, technologies, and evolved psychological mechanisms that work together to suppress or regulate self-interest and make cooperative societies possible...We evolved to live, trade, and trust within shared moral matrices. When societies lose their grip on individuals, allowing all to do as they please, the result is often a decrease in happiness and an increase in suicide." Liberalism has advantages over libertarianism because it acknowledges the moral sphere of harm/care in addition to fairness/proportionality. But humans are groupish as well as empathetic. We need to take into account the importance of loyalty, authority, and religion. This brings us to the third political philosophy, conservatism.

The founder of modern Western conservatism was the Anglo-Irish statesman Edmund Burke. Dismayed by the excesses of the French Revolution, he wrote passionately about the importance of the relationship between individuals and their shared traditions: "we fear God, we look up with awe to kings; with affection to parliaments; with duty to magistrates; with reverence to priests; and with respect to nobility. Why? Because when such ideas are brought before our minds, it is natural to be so affected." Burke recognized that there is an unwritten social contract between citizens and their traditions, no matter how flawed, that cannot simply be swept aside by rational argument, no matter how persuasive, without bloodshed and anarchy. Change should come gradually and consensually; reform is preferable to revolution. The disenfranchised have little to lose (and much to gain) from the overthrow of established norms. They tend to be liberal or libertarian. But those with more moral capital have much to lose (and therefore more to conserve). Those on the right side of the groupish distribution also tend to favor a rightward bias on their graphic equalizer. Although they aren't necessarily wealthy, those who want to conserve moral capital also tend to be fiscally conservative as well, largely because of their desire to preserve the status quo. Conservatives fear radical change that can damage or overturn the moral framework around which they live their lives. They move to the rhythm of the traditions and habits inherited from their forefathers, not because it is necessarily fair or compassionate, but because it's habitual. And the power of habit is not to be underestimated.

The West has a rich and venerable tradition of libertarian liberalism, which, in a rudimentary form, dates back to the Classical Greeks. In contrast, East Asians have been natural born conservatives since before Confucius, as I described in chapter four. But Asians have had their share of revolution. This is because it's natural that in a system without a democratic release valve, the oppression of despotic governments can only go so far before imploding. Not all groups are equally good. It's common wisdom that a good marriage is better than a bad one. But you need to divorce before you can remarry. When push came to shove, as it occasionally did throughout Chinese history, leaders and dynasties were violently overthrown. This reminds me of a message I once found in a fortune cookie: "change comes slowly, except when it comes quickly."

In the last several election cycles, Asian Americans swung more heavily for the Democrats than any other ethnicity except for African Americans. 73% of Asian American voters supported Barack Obama in 2012. This is a dramatic turnaround for a demographic that until the 1992 election trended more reliably Republican than even working class white men. In that election, 55% of Asian Americans voted for George H. W. Bush. How did the Right lose a group so naturally steeped in conservative values? One theory is that the younger generation had Americanized and adopted more liberal ways, perhaps as a deliberate reaction against the stifling conservatism of their elders. But another explanation is that they felt betrayed by the false promises they thought would come their way in the land of endless opportunity. "I thought in America, hard work counted for something," one Korean mother lamented bitterly after her son was passed up by the Ivy League apparently favor of less qualified white legacy kids. You don't have to be liberal to want to kick out the white boys in the country club.

Legacy advantage and other forms of conservative favoritism are not limited to the West. This sort of corruption is far more pervasive in Asia. What's different here is that the bums in charge happen to be of a different race. The solution for Asian Americans is the same for Asians in Asia: people should be treated individually. Asian Americans are not monolithic. Some are economically disadvantaged and deserve affirmative action while others come from privilege and will enjoy legacy advantage once they get their foot in the door. We shouldn't dismantle the system just because white people have created it. We simply have to make sure it's available for Asians too.

Meritocratic libertarianism offers a limited view of human nature. It ignores the moral spheres of compassion and community. Fairness has as much to do with empathy and community as it does with liberty. But empathy can lead to equality of outcome, not just equal opportunity, and that pits it against liberty. Community favors loyalty to authority, often cloaked in religion, and that also puts it in conflict with liberty. Yet both are integral parts of evolved human nature, independent of race. How important is compassion and how important is community in relation to meritocracy when it comes to Asian Americans? Poor Asians could use more empathy. Established Asians want more moral capital. As Asian Americans move up the social ladder and feel more integrated into American culture, I believe conservative values will continue to be important for them.

From Pseudo-Meritocracy to Unique Identity

The white upper-middle classes who pride themselves on their liberal open-minded worldviews are nonetheless responsible for much of the inequality we see in America today by maintaining a cultural barrier to keep out those unlike them. They do this not only by gerrymandering their election districts, zoning their communities, and privatizing their schools, but by lingo, habits, and conventions designed, often subconsciously, to intimidate or discourage outsiders from joining in. As David Brooks wrote in one of his more insightful columns (New York Times, July 11, 2017), "to feel at home in opportunity-rich areas, you've got to understand the right barre techniques, sport the right baby carrier, have the right podcast, food truck, tea, wine and Pilates tastes, not to mention possess the right attitudes about David Foster Wallace, child-rearing, gender norms and intersectionality." The white upper-middle classes may honestly believe they are climbing the socio-economic ladder of meritocracy fair and square. But it is only a local meritocracy. The playing field is rigged to their specifications. The system is gamed. They are hitting their drive shots from the women's tees. Asian Americans by virtue of their outsider status are culturally handicapped from birth. Those who manage to claw their way to the top had to work harder, or lucked out as tokens or arm candy. Asian Americans live in a pseudo-meritocracy.

The journalist Michael Luo, in an open letter published in the New York Times (*An Open Letter to the Woman Who Told My Family to Go Back to China,* October 9, 2016) shares an incident that perfectly captures what all Asian Americans have experienced at some point:

> "...I was with my family and some friends on the Upper East Side of Manhattan. We were going to lunch, trying to see if there was room in the Korean restaurant down the street. You were in a rush. It was raining. Our stroller and a gaggle of Asians were in your way. But I was, honestly, stunned when you yelled at us from down the block, 'Go back to China!...Go back to your fucking country.' 'I was born in this country!' I yelled back. It felt silly. But how else to prove I belonged? Maybe you don't know this, but the insults you hurled at my family get to the heart of the Asian American experience. It's this persistent sense of otherness that a lot of us struggle with every day. That no matter what we do, how successful we are, what

friends we make, we don't belong. We're foreign. We're not American."

The irate upper-middle class woman labeled Luo an outsider from the moment she set her biased eyes on him, without any other information other than perhaps the shape of his eyes. We are seen as outsiders who must somehow "prove" that we belong (by speaking English, eating hot dogs, watching the Super Bowl), while white Americans belong by default.

What then can be done? One approach is to swallow the challenge of the pseudo-meritocracy, handicap and all. "Study twice as hard, kick the SAT in the butt, go to med school, and one day those white trash will be working for you" my dad once told me after the boys at the bus stop called me chink for the 100th time. J. T. Tran espouses an extreme militant version of this approach with his boot camp for under-confident Asian men. This may work for some of the more talented and aggressive Asians, but not for the bulk of them, who will only become more stressed out by self-inflicted pressure of trying to beat the white man at his own game.

The other approach is to re-appropriate what it means to be Asian American, much as African Americans have done with hip-hop culture. The influential Korean American blogger Phil Yu has been instrumental in this development with his internet site, *Angry Asian Man*. This forum encourages Asian Americans of all persuasions, Chinese, Japanese, male, female, liberal, conservative, gay, straight to come together and form a variegated community bonded only by their common pan-Asian heritage. This allows them not just to call out racism when it happens, but to forge a hybrid culture unlike anything in Asia, that is at once American, but not white American, much like what the English, the Germans, the Irish, and the Italians did for themselves over the generations after they settled in the New World, mixed with one another and proudly called themselves "Americans". This new identity, this singular Asian American identity, separate from whatever identities they may have brought over as first generation Korean Americans or Vietnamese Americans or Chinese Americans struggling to make it in a foreign land, then forms a springboard for educating and influencing the non-Asian American society beyond with its unique standards, values, symbols, and mythologies. Only when Asian Americans reclaim their identity from white America, when they can comfortably play by their rules rather than struggle to measure up to white American rules, when Asian Americans create games all Americans embrace, but Asian Americans dominate, only then can we hear someone, anyone scream *"CHINK!!"* at us at the top of their lungs, and not be affected in any way.

Bibliography

ABCs of Attraction/The #1 Dating Bootcamp For Asian Men. www. abcsofattraction.com.

Angry Asian Man. http://blog.angryasianman.com/.

Beevor, Antony. The Second World War. London: Weidenfeld & Nicolson, 2012.

Borshay Liem, Deann. First Person Plural. Sundance Films, 2000.

Borshay Liem, Deann. In the Matter of Cha Jung Hee. PBS, 2010.

Buss, David. The Evolution of Desire: Strategies of Human Mating. New York: Basic Books, 1995.

Chua, Amy. Battle Hymn of the Tiger Mother. London: Penguin, 2011.

Chiao, Joan, S.C. Lee, R. Seligman, and R. Turner (Eds.). Oxford Handbook of Cultural Neuroscience. New York: Oxford University Press, 2016.

Cochran, Gregory, Jason Hardy and Henry Harpending. "Natural History of Ashkenazi Intelligence". Journal of Biosocial Science. 38 (5): 659-693 (2006).

Dawkins, Richard. The Ancestors Tale: A Pilgrimage to the Dawn of Life. London: Weidenfeld & Nicolson, 2004.

Demick, Barbara. Nothing to Envy: Ordinary Lives in North Korea. New York: Spiegel & Grau, 2009.

Diamond, Jared. Guns, Germs, and Steel: The Fates of Human Societies. New York: W. W. Norton, 1997.

Espenshade, Thomas and Alexandria Radford. No Longer Separate, Not Yet Equal: Race and Class in Elite College Admission and Campus Life. Princeton: Princeton University Press, 2009.

Ferguson, Niall. Civilization: The West and the Rest. London: Penguin Press, 2011.

Golden, Daniel. The Price of Admission: How America's Ruling Class Buys Its Way Into Elite Colleges—and Who Gets Left Outside the Gates. New York: Broadway Books, 2007.

Gould, Stephen Jay. The Mismeasure of Man. New York: W. W. Norton & Company, 1981.

Haidt, Jonathan. The Righteous Mind: Why Good People are Divided by Politics and Religion. New York: Pantheon Books, 2012.

Huang, Chi-chung, trans. The Analects of Confucius. Oxford: Oxford University Press, 1997.

Hwang, David Henry. M Butterfly. (1988).

Hyun, Jane. Breaking the Bamboo Ceiling: Career Strategies for Asians. New York: HarperCollins, 2005.

Johnson, Adam. The Orphan Master's Son. New York: Random House, 2012.

Kahneman, Daniel. Thinking Fast and Slow. New York: Farrar, Straus and Giroux, 2011.

Kandel, Eric, James Schwartz and Thomas Jessell. Principles of Neural Science. 5th ed. Amsterdam: Elsevier, 2012.

Kim, Elaine. Dangerous Women: Gender and Korean Nationalism. (co-edited with Chungmoo Choi), New York: Routledge, 1998.

Kim, Eleana. Adopted Territory: Transnational Korean Adoptees and the Politics of Belonging. Durham: Duke University Press, 2010.

Li, Jun, et al. "Worldwide Human Relationships Inferred from Genome-Wide Patterns of Variation". Science. 319 (5866): 1100-1104 (2008).

Miller, Geoffrey. The Mating Mind: How Sexual Choice Shaped the Evolution of Human Nature. New York: Anchor Books, 2000.

Mitchell, Stephen. Tao Te Ching: A New English Version. New York: HarperCollins, 1988.

Murray, Charles. Human Accomplishment: The Pursuit of Excellence in the Arts and Sciences, 800 B.C. to 1950. New York: HarperCollins, 2003.

Nisbett, Richard. The Geography of Thought: How Asians and Westerners Think Differently…and Why. New York: Free Press, 2003.

Peng, Kaiping and Eric Knowles. "Culture and Human Inference: Perspectives from Three Traditions". Handbook of Culture and Psychology. D. Matsumoto, ed. 245-264. Oxford: Oxford University Press, 2001.

Pew Research Asian Americans Survey/Pew Research Center. www.pewsocialtrends.org>asianamericans.

Pinker, Steven. The Blank Slate: The Modern Denial of Human Nature. London: Penguin, 2003.

Pinker, Steven. The Better Angels of Our Nature: Why Violence has Declined. New York: Viking Books, 2011.

Prasso, Sheridan. The Asian Mystique: Dragon Ladies, Geisha Girls, & Our Fantasies of the Exotic Orient. New York: Public Affairs: 2005.

Rawls, John. A Theory of Justice. Cambridge: Harvard University Press, 1971.

Saxe, Rebecca and Nancy Kanwisher. "People Thinking About Thinking People. The Role of the Temporo-parietal Junction in 'Theory of Mind' ". Neuroimage. 19 (4): 1835-1842 (2003).

Schwartz, Robert. "Racial Profiling in Medical Research". New England Journal of Medicine. 344: 1392-1393 (2001).

Tan, Jingze, Yajun Yang, Kun Tang, Pardis Sabeti, Li Jun, Sija Wang. "The Adaptive Variant EDARV370A is Associated with Straight Hair in East Asians". Human Genetics. 132: 1187-1191 (2013).

Tizon, Alex. Big Little Man. Boston: Houghton Miffin Harcourt, 2014.

Veale, David, Sarah Miles, Sally Bramley, Gordon Muir and John Hodsoll. "Am I Normal? A Systematic Review and Construction of Nomograms for Flaccid and Erect Penis Length and Circumference In Up To 15,521 Men". BJU International. 115 (6): 978-986 (2015).

Wade, Nicholas. A Troublesome Inheritance: Genes Race, and Human History. London: Penguin, 2014.

Watson, Burton, trans. The Analects of Confucius. New York: Columbia University Press, 2007.

Witkin, Herman and Solomon Asch. "Studies in Space Orientation: IV. Further Experiments on Perception of the Upright with Displaced Visual Fields". <u>Journal of Experimental Psychology</u>. 38: 762-782 (1948).

Yang, Wesley. "Paper Tigers". <u>New York Magazine</u>. 8 May, 2011.